Lessons From the Startup Trenches
20 Secrets to Entrepreneurial Success

K.C. Hildreth

Copyright © 2017 K.C. Hildreth

Published by Hildreth-Vyas Consulting, Park City, UT

www.kchildreth.com

All rights reserved.

ISBN:
ISBN-13: 978-1978451438
ISBN 10: 1978451431

DEDICATION

To Neha. Your love and support makes everything possible.

ACKNOWLEDGEMENTS

Special thanks to my clients, friends and family. I am very grateful for your unswerving encouragement and support.

OTHER BOOKS BY K.C. HILDRETH

The Evolution of an Ordinary Leader
A Novel

The Power of YOU
Understanding and Unleashing the Incredible Potential Within

Fund Your Dreams!
Proven Tools for Pitching Investors

Supercharge Your Startup!
Creating a Powerful Vision and Business Plan in 5 Easy Steps

Living Into Your Highest Potential
3 Key Steps to Personal Growth

CONTENTS

Preface	i
Introduction	1
Lesson 1: You are Not Alone	3
Lesson 2: Choose Partners Carefully	9
Lesson 3: Your Hires can Make (or Break) Your Company	21
Lesson 4: Culture Determines Success	39
Lesson 5: Don't Ride the Roller Coaster	49
Lesson 6: Believe in Human Potential - Empower Your People	57
Lesson 7: Investors are Everywhere, but Choose Carefully	65
Lesson 8: Execution is Everything (not Your Idea)	75
Lesson 9: Develop Your Persistence Muscle	83
Lesson 10: Learn How to Learn	97
Lesson 11: Cash (flow) is King	109
Lesson 12: An Exit Strategy is a Failure Strategy	119
Lesson 13: Communication Skills are Critical	127
Lesson 14: Lawyers are for Emergencies Only	139
Lesson 15: Get Comfortable with Risk	151
Lesson 16: Transparency = Trust	159
Lesson 17: Align Your Team	169
Lesson 18: Create Alternatives and Options	177
Lesson 19: Watch Your Cap-Table	187
Lesson 20: Become an Inspirational Leader	197
Conclusion	211

PREFACE

This book is one of a series of books on Success, Entrepreneurship, Organizational Culture, and, in the future, many other topics related to human creativity, performance and growth. All of my books are intended as an introduction to topics that can be, and I believe should be, explored in more detail. For ease of access they are purposefully short and easy to digest. I encourage you to test, explore and learn more about each topic so that you can expand upon what I have written. In my work with clients I stress that the process of learning and growing is highly unique to each person and occurs best when *you decide you want to grow*. If you want the knowledge in this book to trigger something, then it will. I can only offer you the processes and information that I know to be effective. I hope it works for you!

If you need help, I am available.

K.C. Hildreth

www.kchildreth.com

INTRODUCTION

Starting a company is probably the most exciting, inspiring, daunting, challenging, frustrating, creative and rewarding thing you will ever do. If you are the type of person that loves to create, has a strong vision, and is willing to be persistent through everything, then there will never be anything so completely absorbing and stimulating. If you like the safety and security of the 'known', however, the start-up world may not be for you. Entrepreneurship will stretch you in every way. You will grow mentally, emotionally and spiritually. If this sounds like something you want, then this book is for you!

To date I have founded, co-founded or advised over 30 start-ups, created multiple new products from within existing companies, and have seen both success and failure in my 30+ years in business. I have experienced virtually every situation that a small enterprise can create, and have come to learn lessons that were both important and, in some cases, painful. In writing this book I hope I can help aspiring entrepreneurs make great decisions, avoid costly mistakes and help YOU create a business that is built for success. You don't need to repeat others' missteps! There are lessons you can learn if you are willing to humble yourself to the process.

This book is organized into a series of lessons. I start with some very high-level concepts that I recommend you internalize before moving to more nuanced ideas. Within each lesson there are 'stories from the trenches' to give you concrete examples from actual situations. Some of these situations I have personally experienced, while others are stories from the many entrepreneurs and investors I have come to know. I have tried to include both inspiring and 'nightmare' stories to give you a good feel for both sides. Needless to say, all names have been changed to protect the innocent! There are no value judgments here, no 'good or bad' actors. There are only effective and ineffective ways of doing things, and these stories are merely guides to help you make informed decisions.

I recommend that you read this book more than once as you grow your company. Some of the lessons are more helpful as you are just starting out, while others can provide warnings and hints that are more applicable as you grow. The start-up process is incredibly dynamic and fast moving, so you will want to watch for the pot-holes and opportunities on an ongoing basis.

Good luck, have fun, and prepare yourself for an incredible journey! You can do anything to which you put your mind…so go for it!

K.C. Hildreth, Park City, UT, July, 2017

LESSON 1: YOU ARE NOT ALONE

In the run-up to the 2012 presidential election Barack Obama made a statement that created political hay for its seeming insensitivity to entrepreneurs. In a speech in Roanoke, VA, he said 'you didn't build that' when referring to the public infrastructure that business owners use to support their operations. The President was referring specifically to the roads, bridges, water, sewer and energy systems that undergird our nation's economy, yet it was reinterpreted by detractors to suggest that he was denying business-owners the respect and accolades they are rightly due. The spin was in full swing.

What was lost, however, is the underlying point. No matter how much you might think you are alone in the process of starting and operating a company, you are not. You are part of a family, a society, and a world that is highly interconnected. In short, you are part of a system that allows you to create success in the world. To deny this system is to believe you are the creator of all things.

When you believe that you are alone, starting a company can be truly overwhelming and stressful. Some of the worst times I have encountered as an entrepreneur have been when I believed that nobody was supporting me...that nobody cared. This feeling creates a sense of loneliness and isolation that made it challenging to get up in the morning, let alone push toward a lofty vision.

On the flip side, this feeling of isolation also creates a kind of megalomania where all good things come from you and nobody else. If the company is successful you take full credit, standing in the limelight declaring that 'you are THE ONE'. This feels great in the moment, but the reality of your aloneness lurks right around the corner. The next time something 'bad' happens, you are back in the dumpster feeling separated and confused.

The truth is that you are never alone and never have been. Every step of the way there are people that have helped you get to WHERE you are. Your family and friends, no matter how dysfunctional, have helped you become WHO you are. The people who oversaw your schooling (traditional or not) taught you how to do what you are doing, even if that happened by example. Your investors helped you get started. Your previous employers helped you save money. Your significant other and friends stick by you. Your customers buy from you, and your vendors sell to you. Your business partners and employees work with you.

You have *never* been alone.

When you *act* like you are alone then you tend to push people away, and this is not good for business. If you sit lamenting how 'nobody understands', then you create that reality. People avoid you and your victim story. As you develop a 'lone-wolf' bitterness you repel anyone who is inclined to help. What you think is 'lonesome reality' is actually a creation of your mind.

When you tell the world you are alone you also become selfish. You claim that you are the creator of all things, and this disempowers those around you. Employees lose their motivation when their leader takes all the credit. When a leader refuses to ask for help because he or she thinks (s)he know everything, then (s)he is essentially telling his/her employees and partners that they are worthless. A leader who claims he or she is alone is not really a leader but an autocrat.

As you start (and most importantly operate) your company, take a moment to notice those around you. See how you are connected to the world. Identify the people in your life that have helped, and then look for those who can help you in the future. How have your family and friends supported you? Your colleagues? Customers? Vendors? Who might be able to help you going forward? Advisors, mentors or consultants? Support groups? Teachers? There are people all around you who can act as resources in your quest. BE GRATEFUL. When you see them, acknowledge them and ask for their participation…they will inevitably add to your success while also giving you a sense of inclusiveness and peace.

Takeaways:

- Humble yourself. Ask for help and advice. Listen. Learn.
- Include people in your decision process. Make everyone feel welcome.
- Look for the ways in which you have been helped. Notice your connectedness.
- Thank everyone in your life. Live in gratitude for the people in your life.
- Take a moment to appreciate those close to you. They don't *have* to be there.
- Give credit easily and often, for everything. Let go of ego. Make others the center of attention.
- Your success is defined by the success of the company and those you work with, not by how often you are in the limelight.

Case 1: Left Out

Steve looked up from his newspaper in disbelief. As a minority founder in a startup Steve knew that he was not the 'top dog', but this was too much. Once again his partner and co-founder was quoted as saying that he was the founder of their company and the main driver behind its success. Sure, Steve thought to himself, John had the initial idea. He deserved more stock and the CEO role. Maybe even more credit. But there were three other co-founders who made his idea real. Wasn't that worth at least a mention? Some sort of acknowledgement?

Talking to him later, Steve confided that this was the final straw for him. "I just felt like I didn't exist. John seemed obsessed with his own legacy and refused to acknowledge anyone but himself. He even stopped inviting us to important meetings! I can't tell you how depressing that felt, after all the work I had put in." Shortly after this episode Steve and the other minority co-founder left the company. The investors were shocked and began to question the future of the enterprise. "No amount of pay or stock was worth how I felt," Steve shrugged. "I learned a lot, but will be much more careful about who I associate with in the future."

Case 2: Giving Props

Tom, Michael and Carolyn sat in their 4th investor meeting in 3 days. They were getting good at the process, encouraging each other and pitching the idea with increasing intensity. Tom, being the initial founder, CEO and largest shareholder, would start each pitch by extolling the virtues of his co-founders. He would speak enthusiastically about having 'the smartest people in the country' involved in this project. Michael and Carolyn would blush with embarrassment at the glowing sentiments, but also felt a tremendous positive energy building inside themselves.

As Michael later related, "I felt almost high from what Tom said. By the time I got up to present my piece I was so confident and inspired that I blew the investors out of the water. After each success Tom would 'high-five' us for our great presentations. I know it sounds silly, but it really meant something. I felt like we were unstoppable." During that same fund-raising tour Tom, Carolyn and Michael raised over $50 million dollars and went on to build a successful company in a very difficult industry. After the company was acquired (with a profit to all investors), all of the founders and top leaders declared it <u>the best management team they had ever been a part of</u>.

LESSON 2: CHOOSE PARTNERS CAREFULLY

As you can tell from the previous lesson, a partner or partners can have a substantial effect on your energy and drive. I have had the good fortune to work with some great partners in my ventures, people who provided inspiration, knowledge, skills and support, especially when things were not going well. A bad partner, in contrast, can drain you and pull you down even in the best of times. Your job is to be very selective and, contrary to the optimism I usually preach, somewhat critical. When you start a company with another person you are essentially getting married. You must treat the process with just as much importance as you would when choosing a mate.

I have worked with many entrepreneurs over the past 30 years and can tell you that one of the most cringe-inducing statements a founder can utter is: "I am thinking of bringing my friend on as a partner. I have known him (or her) for a long time and think that (s)he will be fun to work with." Even worse, "My spouse and I have decided to start a company. I think it would be good for us!" When I hear these statements I immediately picture the detritus of broken friendships, lost relationships, and acrimonious separations.

I don't mean to be overly pessimistic here, but I have seen so many dysfunctional startup relationships that it is hard not to err on the side of caution. I have seen lawsuits, screaming matches, and in one case watched one partner almost throw a chair at another. People stop speaking with each other, quit unexpectedly, form competing camps inside the company, and actually work to destroy the company from the inside out in order to deny their partner the satisfaction of success. It is insanity personified, and results from strong personalities interacting in never-ending, high-pressure situations.

Picture three opinionated people trapped in a cabin over a long winter. Then add 18-hour workdays and high-pressure deadlines. Now slowly reduce their supplies of food and water. Within months even the most easy-going and persistent people will begin to crack. This is why NASA screens so heavily for space missions. Without adequate screening space travel would quickly become a murderous experience!

It is not only difficult circumstances that can generate friction…success does as well. I have seen partners and investors (normally very nice people) become vicious when a lot of money is on the table. Interactions can devolve into a selfish, winner-take-all mentality where people forget that they are supposed to be friends.

In the business world this free-for-all is the playground of litigation attorneys seeking for their next big payoff. Selfishness can litigate every penny out of a successful enterprise.

My point is to *pick your partners carefully*. If you pick well you dramatically increase your chances of success. If you don't you can kill your business faster than any mismanagement or poor strategy ever will. You must always remember that your business is first and foremost a *social enterprise*. Behind every vision, strategy, operation and service lie *people*. Without good people working together in a constructive way you cannot succeed in business - period. This applies not just to your partners, but to your employees (the subject of a later lesson).

When working with entrepreneurs I recommend they treat potential partnership discussions as 'self-unveilings'. Each person needs to openly explore their fears, doubts, desires, as well as their strengths and weaknesses. Both people must be willing to communicate in a way that creates mutual trust, and be willing to walk away if it does not feel right. The key, in my experience, is the *ability to communicate openly and respectfully*. Listening is critical. When two people are willing to say and hear anything, then building a business becomes a process of creating value. When two people are not willing to speak openly and kindly, then the friction that results will suck value out of the enterprise.

Your friend may be loyal but not good with money. Your spouse might be loving yet unreliable. Your colleague can be good at her job and yet not built for the stress of a startup. You must find these things out *before* you start a company. I can tell you that waiting for 1-2 years to find out that you and your partner are not a 'fit' is a very painful thing!

In order to create understanding, here are some questions I recommend prospective partners ask each other before they commit (and periodically throughout the life of the company):

- What is your communication style?
- What is your communication style under stress?
- How do you handle conflict?
- What is your risk tolerance? (VERY important)
- How long would you be willing to go with no income?
- When would you feel the need to 'call it quits'?
- What are you willing to give up for the enterprise?
- What does it mean to you to commit to something?
- What do you love to do?
- What are your greatest skills?
- How can you be most successful in this company?
- What is your vision for this company? What do you want to create?
- What drives you as a person?
- Are you willing to tell the microscopic truth about everything?
- What are your greatest fears? What do you worry about?

- What does it mean to have a meaningful life?
- Why are you doing this?
- How much time are you willing to dedicate to this?
- How are we going to make decisions? What if we disagree?
- Would you ever want to sell the venture?
- What type of people do you like to be around?
- What is your greatest concern about me?

As you can see the list of questions is incredibly thorough. However, the toughest part of these conversations is interpreting the answers. For example, many people in a potential startup situation will say they have a high risk tolerance when in reality they don't, or at least don't understand what 'risk' means. A person can see themselves as 'a risk taker', only to quickly back away when confronted with a few months of unpaid work, or the prospect of going into debt. Your job is to listen carefully and observe behavior over words. If your potential partner has never quit a job to start something new, never left their home town, or does not travel much, then you will want to question their tolerance for risk. I also recommend talking to the spouse/significant other of your partner. If your partner's spouse becomes 'freaked out' about the level of risk being taken, then you can be sure that your partner will be forced to choose one or the other…and most likely it will be their relationship over your business (as is should be).

Which brings me to the concept of a partner. Generally, there are two types of people in the work world today. First, there are the people who see themselves as 'employees'. These are people who speak about 'the powers that be'. Employees see themselves as part of a structure that is safe, known and hierarchical. And to be clear, these are not just the 'lower ranks'. Many leaders in large organizations see themselves as cogs as well. They talk about bosses, career paths and bonus structures. Everything is about the paycheck and the retirement plan. These people *are not entrepreneurs.*

Natural entrepreneurs tend to see themselves as self-employed by nature. They do not acknowledge structures and generally believe that anything can be accomplished with creativity and drive. To say 'I can't' is anathema to the partner of a startup. A genuine entrepreneur understands risk and is willing to sacrifice in the short term in order to accomplish a greater goal. Whereas an employee might ask 'how much am I going to get paid?', a startup partner will ask 'what ownership percentage will I have?'. The founders of a startup know that they are betting on themselves, and are willing to put all the chips on the table for a larger payoff in the end. To an entrepreneur a paycheck is nothing compared to the thrill and potential benefit of creating something huge.

There is nothing right or wrong with being either one or another of these types of people. Yet it is very important to know how your partner looks at things. I have personally made the mistake of selecting a 'BIG NAME from a MAJOR FIRM' on as a founder or leader, only to see them become extremely uncomfortable in the startup environment. *Being highly accomplished and educated does not mean a person is entrepreneurial!* I once tried to help a former executive (picture COO/CEO) from a large firm start his own company. He could not handle the fact that when he made phone calls people would not call him back. This man was used to *deference* and *power*. He need the structure and title of an organization. He was an *employee*, not an entrepreneur.

Ideally, your partner should also be different from you. You want a partner to have skills that compliment yours. If you are outgoing and good at sales, for example, then you want your partner to be structured and internally focused. If you are highly technical, then you want a person with creative or people skills. If you are highly energetic, then you might want someone a bit more calm and level-headed. The key is to find someone with a mix of attributes and skills that allows you to create more than you could create alone. 1 + 1 = 3. Synergy.

No matter how different you are, however, you must have three things in common. First, you must be able to communicate openly, transparently, respectfully and often. If you cannot do this, it really does not matter how close your skills 'fit' because you won't be able to share enough to make them relevant. This is true of any relationship. Without close communication there is no connection. There is no way to apply the benefits of diversity.

Second, you must have a shared commitment to the vision. As partners you must see the same future for yourselves and the company, and commit to it without reservation. This is true for everyone in the company, but it is especially true for the founders. I recommend having an ongoing process whereby you share how you see things and probe into details in order to clarify discrepancies. It is very easy to overlook differences in vision. As social creatures we want to agree. We want to get along and assume the best. *Do not fall into this trap.* Find the differences of opinion and talk through them respectfully and openly. Compromise and get creative. Find new ways of looking at things. In the end, you must come to a consensus around what you are creating. Without a shared vision you are setting yourself up for conflict and inefficiency. With a powerful, shared partnership vision you can create anything.

Last, it is extremely important that you and your partner share basic life values. Inevitably you will hit difficult situations in one form or another. How do you treat others in those moments? Do you truly value people and care about them? How will you talk to each other? What are your principles and how do you live them? Do you walk the walk? Having a shared set of core values can go a long way in tough moments. Widely divergent values can create misunderstanding, conflict and ultimately, an inability to work together.

Key Takeaways:

- A dysfunctional founding team cannot work its way out of a paper bag. A well constructed founding team can create amazing things while dominating the market. Your partner *matters*.

- Be choosy about who you work with. Set up evaluation parameters and stick to them.
- Just because you like someone does not make them a business partner.
- If you are going to commit to a partnership, commit fully and completely.
- Set up a communication process that promotes continued openness. Ask each other the difficult questions. Probe for differences and contradictions.
- Evaluate someone both on what they say and how they act. What they do will tell you more than what they say. Look for inconsistency.
- Employees do not make good founders (except on rare occasions).
- Your founding team must be able to 1) communicate openly and often, and 2) share a common vision (right down to the details).
- Know your own core values and look for partners that share those same values.

Partnership 1: Best of Friends

Paul and Stefan had been friends for a long time. They attended college together, travelled occasionally, and were roommates on and off. Both were successful in their own fields, so when they decided to start a clothing business together it seemed to be a no-brainer. "Paul is a detail-oriented task master, and I am a natural people person," Stefan said later, "so it looked like we were a perfect match." As time went on, however, Stefan began to notice things about Paul that he had never seen. "Paul took on a controlling, secretive style," Stefan recalled. "I wasn't sure if I could trust him anymore. And I don't think he trusted me either."

As time went on Paul began to accuse Stefan of trying to take over the company while Stefan increasingly saw Paul as manipulative and duplicitous. The atmosphere became toxic as the two refused to speak openly to one another. Employees could feel the tension, and all communication was eventually turned over to private attorneys who slowly drained their personal accounts. In the end, neither Paul nor Stefan made much money. "I look back on that time and just cringe," Stefan admitted after everything was over. "My child was born over those years, yet I spent virtually every moment of his young life obsessing over my business partnership. I don't know what happened. I just wish I had known Paul better." Stefan and Paul are no longer friends and have not spoken in years.

Partnership 2: Commitment to the Process

Gene called Thomas with tension in his voice. He was about to finalize the partnership agreements and needed to know if Thomas was fully on board to start this company. "I was having pangs of doubt," Gene recalled, "I needed to know once and for all if Thomas was going to be a reliable partner. I did not know him outside of his glowing recommendations and our initial conversations. His skill-set matched mine, but I had no idea of his commitment level." Thomas, for his part, was a seasoned entrepreneur who knew what it was going to take to build a successful company. "When Gene called," Thomas recounted, "I knew exactly what he was asking. I would have asked the same questions myself. He was the main founder and needed minority partners who were going to stay with him through the thick-and-thin."

During the conversation Thomas listened to Gene's questions and then cut right to the point. "I stopped Gene at one point and called everything out on the table. I told him I understood his concerns and believed that he was right to be worried. He did not know me from Adam. Then I told him that under no uncertain terms I would be there to turn the lights out with him if it came to that. I said I could support myself for at least 7 months without salary and that I would put everything I had into the company. I held nothing back." Gene recalled the conversation later, saying "I knew at that moment that this was my partner. He was so utterly committed that I knew we would make it." In the end, Gene and Thomas sold their company for over $100 million. Looking back, both founders recall the forming of their partnership as one of the most powerful times of their lives.

LESSON 3: THE PEOPLE YOU HIRE CAN MAKE (OR BREAK) YOUR COMPANY

If you have ever interviewed with a large company you know that most well run firms have an extensive and detailed hiring process. It is not uncommon for a market-leading company to require 6-7 rounds of interviews, personality tests, drug tests, and case-based sample work assignments. From the outside the level of scrutiny might seem overbearing and unnecessary. What these top firms know, however, is that *hiring matters*. Bringing in a high-performer who fits well in the company culture can result in a significant boost to the bottom line. On the other hand, hiring a low-performing, trouble-making individual can cost a company by some estimates upwards of $500,000. As all Human Resources managers know, a company is made up of *people*. People will determine the success of the organization…and can just as assuredly doom it to failure.

The role of any individual in the success of a company is especially true for a start-up. When a company is small, any one individual has a proportionately larger impact on the group than if the person's energy were diffused among a larger organization. Each time you hire you will be changing the dynamic of your company, and so you must look at each potential employee as a *founder* who will determine the success or failure of the enterprise. The IT person you bring in to support your internal computer network can have just as much influence on your operation as a senior executive in a larger firm. *Everyone* you hire in the first two years could eventually be an executive. You must consider each person almost as carefully as you would consider a founding partner. Ultimately, you want to hire natural leaders, those that are capable of growing with your company. And by leader we don't mean just a 'title'. Everyone you hire can and should be a leader regardless of their formal position.

It is tempting as an entrepreneur to overlook the importance of hiring, mainly because you are so darn *busy*. I have experienced the stress of seemingly unmanageable workloads, and I have been tempted to hire the first person who promised to help me lighten the load. When you are drowning in work almost everyone seems like a lifeguard. Hiring becomes an act of desperation more than analysis. Rather than wait for the right person you tend to react rather than think, hoping that this earnest, excited applicant will be the answer to your prayers. Yet this almost never works, and the end result can be extremely costly.

No matter what the size of your company or the state of your workload I recommend a rigorous and thorough hiring process (this includes your 'hiring' of a vendor as well. Vendors can be as helpful…and destructive…as anyone you hire). As a leader of your company you may think that your primary role is to make and sell your product or service. And to an extent this is true. You are in the business to sell goods and services for a profit. But you must also understand that of equal importance is your role as a *leader of a group of people*. Without a strong, cohesive, talented group of individuals working as team you cannot grow beyond a certain point. Business is first and foremost a *social enterprise*, and so as a founder of a company one of your primary responsibilities is to hire, grow and care for the source of your future success. You cannot delegate hiring to others. You must take a personal and intense interest in every person that joins your team.

The key to a powerful hiring process lies in the perspectives you gather as you talk to a potential new recruit. Every individual you interview will have multiple 'faces' that they show to the world. The face you see in the interview room will be one that is created for your benefit. This person wants to work for you, and will show you what they think you want to see. But behind that mask lies the *real* person, and it is your job to find out who that is. This is why large companies spend so much time and money testing and interviewing…they want to find out the truth about the people they consider hiring.

It is not only the person being hired who wears a mask. Each person in the interviewer role will also be playing a role that will skew the interpretation of the interview. For example, you may be playing 'CEO and thought leader' who does more selling than probing, while another founder probes for specific skills. Your HR rep may be trying to impress the person in order to fill a position that is desperately vacant. In each case the interviewer will come away with a different 'take' that can be wildly inaccurate if the interviewer and interviewee are both wearing a mask. As a leader your job is to create a process that sees through the masks on both sides. You must seek the *truth* in order to make an informed decision. To do this, I have found it helpful to create an environment that is comfortable and welcoming (versus tense or intimidating), because you will learn more about a person if they feel that they can be themselves. People have interview personalities. That isn't what you're hiring. You're hiring the actual person.

In my experience getting at the truth doesn't necessarily mean a battery of tests or endless interviews. You can do this simply by assigning roles to each interviewer, asking probing, open-ended questions, and listening carefully to the answers. Nobody can (or wants to) hide their true face forever. If you take enough time you can find out virtually anything…as any good detective will attest. In order to ensure that you get the best candidates possible, I recommend the following general process:

1. Clearly define the role. Each open space in your company should come with a detailed description of the activities and responsibilities for the role, and a list of the skills and

requirements necessary to be successful. Continue to refine this role as you go through the process. Often times you learn a lot by interviewing people. That can help shape the role.

2. Define the ideal candidate. Describe the skills, temperament, and abilities that would be found in the 'perfect person'. You are looking for the one in a million candidate, so *be picky*. If you want someone to work long hours without complaint, say so! Ask for what you want!

3. Gather resumes. Place listings with on-line job placement services (colleges, tech outlets, craigslist, etc.) Be prepared to get at least 50 resumes for each position. Ideally, you want 100. Also network with known and trusted contacts. Some of the best candidates come from people who know you and what you need (like co-workers, friends and colleagues).

4. Select top 10-15 candidates for a phone interview. I know it sounds crazy to get 300 resumes when you only need 10 candidates, but if you are going to get the best you must invest the time. This phase is very important and must be done by people who know what they are looking for. As COO of a small company I personally handled this process. You are looking for the 'diamonds in the rough'.

5. Conduct the phone interview. If you are a 2-4 person company, you must conduct this interview yourself. If you are larger, then you might have the person who is hiring do the first phone screen. The phone interview generally looks

for communication skills, basic trust (i.e. truth of the resume) and a confirmation of the overall skillset.

6. Select 3-6 of the successful phone interviews for a first round of in-person talks. This round should be conducted by people who will be working alongside the candidate, and include mainly technical and interpersonal views (see below). Special Note*** If you are not an expert in a position you have to hire, interview more people. You will learn more about the role as you talk to people who have done it.

7. Once the first round is complete, gather all interviewers together and have an open discussion. Encourage each person to speak in-turn and then open the dialogue for debate. The goal is not to decide, but to discover information that might have previously been missed. You are trying to add 'color' to the applicant so that a more complete picture can be drawn.

8. After the group discussion, it will become apparent who makes it to the final round. You may select all - or none - but it is imperative to be extremely picky. Call each of the finalists and invite them for a final round with the founders and, if applicable, executives.

9. During the final round you, as the founder, should be a central part of the interview process. In this round you are looking to dive deeper into the background of the candidate, looking for cultural, interpersonal or temperament 'fit' or 'red flags'. Also in this round one person, ideally you, should give

a 'pitch' about the company to get the candidates excited. When each candidate leaves the office, (s)he should feel very special to have been selected and be very excited to get the job.

10. Check references! Call and interview the references of each finalist. Look for any hesitation on the part of the referral. If possible, find people who are *not* formal references. An independent (ie, not a friend) former colleague of the applicant will give a much better picture of what it is like to work with this person.

11. Make a final decision. Most good companies work on consensus. My experience tells me not to hire unless *everyone* is 'thumbs up'. Even if only one person has a 'thumbs down', then there is usually a good reason why. You must trust your team and their collective 'guts'.

12. Make an offer. If you have found a candidate that works, make a 'contingent offer'. This offer is to work for 3 months for a set rate of pay, with a final offer to come at the end of this period. No matter how 'senior' the person is, or how desirable the candidate seems to be, *always* hire with a contingent offer. More on this below.

As suggested above, I recommend establishing roles or 'views' for each interviewer. Some of these roles may be held by one person, but each should be covered at least once by someone. For example:

1. Technical. This interviewer should be well versed in the technical or process requirements for the job. (S)he should know what it takes to be successful in the job, and be able to tell if the candidate is capable or is 'bluffing'.
2. Cultural. Every company has cultural values, even if they are not stated. This interviewer should write down the values and ask questions designed to uncover the candidate's cultural fit. If one of the values for the company is 'openness', for example, then this interviewer should ask questions designed to identify times when the candidate was open or closed with information. Prevaricating or hiding the truth would be a 'red-flag' in this case.
3. Interpersonal. Likeability is important to any group. People want to like who they are working with. This does not necessarily mean that the candidate needs to be outgoing and funny, but they need to generally fit in. This interviewer can focus on questions that build a picture of the candidate as a human being, identifying markers that indicate social adaptability.
4. Background. In every interview the candidate is presenting the interviewer with an idealized version of their background. There is nothing wrong with this, and should not be looked upon with cynicism. We all want people to see the best of us. This interviewer's job is merely to dive deeper into the candidate's background to look for the red flags that might

indicate a major breach of trust or an inability to work well with others.

5. Temperament. Each role and company comes with a certain 'risk profile'. Some jobs are very predictable and secure, while others are more risky and performance based. This interviewer's job is to determine if the candidate has the temperament for a particular role. If your company is a small startup, for example, you need people who have a flexible, open and risk accepting style.

6. Pitch-person. The interview process is, in a way, also a marketing process. Every person that comes through your doors will go home and talk about your company. So when each candidate leaves they should be terrifically excited at the possibility of your company. They should be *dying* to work for you and with you. Even if they don't get the job, you want them to say "wow, what a great place to work". There should always be one person, preferably the founder, who can paint a glorious picture of the future of your company!

Each interviewer should also be well versed in the process of asking open-ended questions. An open-ended question is one that cannot be answered with a 'yes' or 'no'. It is quite common for an interviewer to talk endlessly about the job and their role. This is a huge mistake. Interviews are places to *learn*, not to *speak* (with the exception of the 'pitch' person). A smart candidate will actually encourage the interviewer to speak because (s)he knows that a) (s)he can learn the best way to get the job, and b) that (s)he cannot incriminate themselves if they are not speaking. There is an old maxim that says, 'The smartest person in the room is usually the one who is not talking'. This is especially true when it comes to interviewing.

Most candidates, and for that matter most human beings, have things they prefer not to be known. In psychological terms this is called the 'Shadow Self'. This self has done or thought things that they find embarrassing and shameful, and therefore seek to hide that part of themselves. Common 'shadow self' topics include secret desires, personality tendencies, hidden angers/resentments and destructive habits. Nothing about the shadow self is actually 'bad' per se. It is simply a part of us that we seek to hide because we think others will judge it.

These hidden parts of a person can, however, impact the effectiveness of that person in their job or role. If a candidate has a secret desire to collect and hoard cat posters, no big deal. But if a candidate has a tendency toward kleptomania, or has a rage issue, or uses alcohol destructively, then you must find this out. Even more subtly, if a candidate harbors resentment toward authority or sees the world in an adversarial way, then (s)he can undermine the culture in ways that eventually turn highly destructive.

Now, most of us think that we can see a person's 'shadow self' fairly easily. An alcoholic is easy to spot, right? My experience tells me that this is not true. As human beings we have developed elaborate mechanisms to hide those parts of ourselves we deem unworthy, and so each candidate will be well aware of his/her own 'red flags' that he/she feels a need to hide. All this person needs is an interviewer who talks more than listens and they are home free. Your job, as the interviewer, is not to let that happen.

I want to be clear that red flags are *not* an opportunity to judge. You have no right to condemn or look down upon anyone's shadow self. If you take a moment to look internally you will see that you too have some things you would rather not share. There are, however, behaviors and tendencies that the company needs to look for in order to create a thriving business. These red flags include:

- General resentment of authority
- A victim mentality (blaming)
- Lack of interest in the content of the role
- Past unresolved conflicts
- Negative, repeated patterns
- A pessimistic outlook on life (especially for a startup)
- Quick to irritation or anger
- Avoidance of truth or openness
- Deep, unresolved fears
- Ongoing complaints and negative storytelling
- Lack of successful outcomes or completions

Again, none of these red flags make the person a bad human being. They simply mean that your job as an employer can become strained and difficult if you have to manage some of these personality tendencies. A person who tells victim or blame stories, for example, can become the very person who sues the company when fired for lack of performance. I have personally made this mistake and, in retrospect, cannot believe I missed the obvious signs.

As I close this chapter, I want to emphasize again the importance of being selective. Hiring the wrong person can be one of the biggest nightmares a small company can face. Inefficiencies, lack of productivity, ongoing disciplinary meetings and lawsuits are all things that can kill a small company or, at the very least, eat away at your organization's culture. A great person can do the opposite. A high performer with strong leadership qualities can increase sales, lift the spirit of the culture, and change the prospects for success. Your job is to find the latter and avoid the former.

To sum it all up, I encourage you to set up a strong process, asked detailed questions, listen carefully to the answers, build consensus and then, in the end, pick the one candidate that your 'gut' tells you is the right person. You will still make mistakes, but the probability of a disastrous hire will be greatly diminished and, hopefully, not repeated.

Key Takeaways:

- Every individual you bring into your company will have an effect on your future.
- It is tempting in times of need to take anyone who comes along.

- Bringing in the wrong person costs you much more than you think.
- Create processes that ensure adequate vetting of any potential hire (or vendor).
- BE PICKY! Especially in the beginning.
- Hire only leaders and those that can grow to bigger leadership roles.
- Take off your 'rose colored glasses' and try to understand your interviewees. Find out who they *really* are, not who you *hope* they are. Create an interview environment that makes that possible.
- Listen more than you speak! You can inspire candidates later…learn about them first!
- Your primary job is to lead a company of people. Choose the people who can help you be successful!

Case 1: The Superstar Executive

The executive team of a small technical startup was so excited they could not stop talking about their good fortune. Steve Jones, a high level executive from a large, powerful conglomerate, had approached them about a position in the company. THE Steve Jones! The PR would be amazing! The startup was doing well and gaining recognition, so the executive team was not surprised that such big names were attracted to their mission. Yet the team was torn. They did not want to put Steve through too much of an interview process lest they scare him away, but they also wanted to make sure he would be easy to work with. In the end they agreed that they would shorten the vetting process significantly, mitigating the risk by dedicating one particularly people-oriented executive to be his 'handler'.

Within a month of Steve joining the company, however, it became clear that they had bitten off more than they could chew. This 'superstar executive' barged into technical meetings, jumped on conference calls unannounced, and publicly berated customers for their 'stupidity'. Steve's handler, an executive with significant responsibilities herself, was forced to spend the vast majority of her time just trying to control his behavior. After one year of Steve's employment the company had lost 2 customers, 3 employees and was engaged in legal negotiations to secure his departure. In the end the executives calculated that this one decision had cost the company over $600,000 in cash and lost business. The executive team found out later that Steven had a pattern of this behavior at previous companies and that not one of his former colleagues were surprised by the outcome.

Case 2: Big Company Blues

As co-founder of a small tech startup Josh knew that hiring was important. He had seen disasters before and was determined not to repeat his mistakes. His other partners, however, were a bit less concerned about the quality of the people and were open to a much broader range of potential hires. So when Josh interviewed a customer account manager from a large multinational corporation, he knew he was going to have a problem. The applicant was skilled, to be sure, but Josh also suspected that he was not going to be ready for the stress and uncertainty that comes with working for a startup.

Given his reticence, Josh painted the worst possible picture of start-up life. He talked about the financial ups and downs, the long hours and the dynamic, shifting environment. He stressed the need for flexibility around the role, and asked repeatedly if the candidate understood what it was going to take to be successful in their new company. Each time the applicant said 'yes' and expressed excitement. Josh, however, was not convinced. He had seen this before. Large-company employees seemed to have a romantic notion that startup life was fun and dynamic and all the things their current job was not. But Josh knew that in the tradeoff between excitement and security, most people would choose security every time. Josh felt this candidate was one of those people.

Josh's partners, however, were enamored with the brand cache of the applicant. They liked having someone from ACME Corp on the team, and so overruled Josh and made the hire. As Josh predicted, within 3 weeks the candidate began to object to the long hours and the tasks that were 'beneath him'. Two months later he quit, leaving Josh to explain to confused customers how their 'new superstar hire' was no longer with the company. Josh vowed never again to let himself be overridden so easily.

Case 3: Patience is a Virtue

Ron reflected on the recent 10 interviews he had conducted. The role was a mid-level management position in software development, but he could tell from the candidates that they were not going to get him where he needed to go. As co-founder and COO, Ron was tasked with building an efficient software production operation that created high-quality output both on-time and within budget. These mid-level managers might help this process, but they certainly were not going to revolutionize the operation.

Given his realization, Ron decided to raise the level of the position to one of significant leadership immediately under him. Even though the company was small, Ron knew that the right person could create significant value. Ron also knew, however, that he was going to have to be patient. These types of superstars did not come along every day. Under a great amount of pressure from both the board and his partner, Ron continued to wait for 9 months until he found someone he thought was good enough for the role. In the end, this new hire completely transformed the company and became a C-level executive that helped bring the company's valuation to over $300 million.

Interviewed later, Ron reflected "This one hiring decision was the best move I have made in my career as an entrepreneur. I am so glad I waited, because if I had acted prematurely I might have missed this key hire entirely. It pays to be patient, it really does!"

Case 4: Process Discipline

Andrea sat looking at the stack of resumes on her desk. She had already looked at 150+ people and had only found 3 potential candidates. Given her leadership team's focus on hiring she knew that even these 3 would likely not make it past the second round. As the new HR manager she had never seen anything like it. The leadership team of this startup was obsessive about finding the right people, and it was looking like she would never be able to fill this software developer role. And this was an entry-level position! What was she going to do with more senior hires?!

Over the next two weeks Andrea, with help from one of the co-founders, read over 1,000 resumes and spoke to 20 people. 5 of those made it in for an interview, and only 2 went to the second round. Yet these two people, she realized, were good. Even better, both were extremely excited to work for the company. The process had been so thorough that each candidate felt like (s)he was interviewing with a truly exceptional company.

After the second round of interviews a large meeting was held in which every interviewer was present. The executive team, the software managers and the software developers all came together to discuss each candidate. Over the next hour each person weighed in on their impressions and challenged each other's assumptions. After much debate, the CEO decided to bring both candidates back for a private lunch with his leadership team. In the end, the decision was made to hire both people.

Looking back Andrea shook her head in amazement. "I had never experienced such seriousness about hiring," she said. And yet, "it really paid off. One of the new hires did work that completely bested our competition and re-wrote the book on what we thought was possible. The guy was a genius with code! And he was easy to work with as well! Nice, easy to manage, articulate, technically brilliant, a culture fit, everything! I learned so much through the process, and will take it wherever I go.

LESSON 4: CULTURE DETERMINES SUCCESS

The moment you and your partner (or your first hire) meet, you are creating a culture. When two people interact they have two conversations: One that is explicit (about the content) and one that is subliminal (about the agreed upon rules and values). The explicit conversation is *verbal*. Words are used to convey meaning from the speaker to the listener, and vice-versa. The subliminal conversation is non-verbal, or *visual*. In this case the participants observe each other's behaviors, tones, facial expressions and implicit meanings in order to come to an agreement upon how future interactions will take place. This agreement is rarely explicit because it happens so quickly and without conscious thought.

When two or more people subliminally agree on 'how to be' with each other, they create a culture. This culture sets rules, establishes values and determines the 'feel' of the group. Anyone who has travelled to another country, especially one that is significantly different from one's own, understands immediately the nature of culture. When we experience an unfamiliar cultural situation we feel out of place, adrift in our own misunderstanding. Nothing seems familiar as we are forced to learn new ways of 'getting along'. Eventually we learn 'how things are done' in this new human organization and find ways of adapting to 'fit in'. Culture is, in short, a human 'operating system' that allows us to interact with each other in a known and predictable way.

So when you and your business partner are having your first meetings, you are establishing a culture that will live as long as your organization lives. Your particular culture will be a combination of both people's 'meta culture' (i.e. your country), your individual cultural backgrounds (i.e. your ethnicity, religion, and country of origin), your local context (i.e. your region or town), your birth/childhood culture (i.e. family), and a myriad of other value-oriented factors. If both of you have vastly different cultural backgrounds, then it might take some time to establish a 'shared culture'. If you are similar or there is one person who is dominant, then it might happen quickly. If your core values are different it can lead to really intense disagreements and a cultural divide. Either way, your culture will be directly influenced by each member of your organization.

Every time you add someone to your company you will be adding to the culture. Each new individual, no matter how 'low' in the company, will bring their cultural background to the mix. The company feel will change and morph constantly as you grow and evolve. This is why hiring is so critical. Hiring a toxic person can literally poison the culture and create endless unintended consequences. Hiring a high performer who is a 'fit' can improve and enrich the culture, adding significantly to an organization's effectiveness. As the culture goes, so goes the performance.

In short: *Your culture is the source of everything that your company produces. In order to build a successful company, you must first build a successful culture.*

In my experience most unseasoned entrepreneurs pay little to no attention to culture as they build their organizations. This is understandable. Small groups of people working toward a common purpose tend to have a performance mentality that can be defined as a 'start-up culture'. The feeling of shared purpose is so powerful that there is no need to discuss what is happening…it just is.

Until the company begins to grow.

As more people join and roles become more defined, pockets of behavior begin to surface. Some people might not work as hard as others. Or one salesperson might decide that being 100% truthful is not necessary. One leader wants to make as much money as possible, while another is trying to build a 'family workplace'. Differences show up, resulting in cultural confusion.

On the other side, common behaviors also begin to appear. Political maneuvering may become systemic as the notion of 'every man for himself' takes hold. Cheating, lying or greed can infest an organization like lice...once present they are very difficult to remove. Many entrepreneurs can relate stories where the founding team eventually looks at each other and asks 'how in the world did we get *here!?*'

A toxic culture can kill a company. People become cynical and tense, which is reflected in both the work product and customer relationships. Employees begin to grumble not only to each other, but also to customers, partners and, worse, on on-line posting boards. When the company tries to raise additional funds each potential investor (as well as existing investors) can easily find out what it is really like to work at the company, and this can be a deal killer.

The bottom line is that your culture matters – a lot. So if you want to create a powerful, productive company you MUST focus on the values and rules that support effectiveness and joy. Most entrepreneurs assume that their 'startup mentality' will become the company culture, and so are surprised when something different arises. In the end many entrepreneurs don't recognize the company they have built, because in many ways it is *not* the company they have built: It is the company the *culture* has built.

The answer, then, is to focus on culture very early in the startup process. I encourage entrepreneurs to have a "values conversation" during the very first days, and to continue that conversation as each person joins. In this conversation the following questions should be answered:

- What are we creating?
- What do we want it to feel like to work at our company?
- What values do we hold as important?
- How do we want to interact with each other?
- What rules would we like to establish?
- What is acceptable (and unacceptable) behavior?
- What is the culture *now*?
- Is the current culture what we want it to be?
- Are there any cultural attributes that are hidden or unsaid?

These questions need to be asked constantly, because a divergent culture can develop quite quickly behind the scenes. All it takes is a few people not 'walking the talk' and the culture can slide into something unintended. One of the key questions is the last: Is there anything hidden or unsaid? Typically I find that there are two views on culture in an organization: The *stated* and the *actual*. For example, the leadership team may say "We value honesty, openness, and work-life balance". When an employee *experiences* the company, however, they find out that the actual culture is "deceit, opacity, and endless hours". This is called 'cultural dissonance', and if left unaddressed can result in a catastrophic breakdown in trust.

In the end, creating a powerful culture is about *conscious conversation*. When people come together and discuss openly what they perceive, want and value then they develop a bond. Even if they don't agree on everything they hear what others value and relate to them in that space. Trust is built and a harmonic culture ensues. If you want to create a powerful culture, then you must start early, talk often, and dedicate yourselves to building a system that works well into the future.

I have found that companies that build powerful cultures rarely worry about theft, dishonesty, conflict, grumbling, complaining or any other inefficient activity. They don't worry because in a great, cohesive culture it is unthinkable to do any of these things. It simply does not occur to an employee to be lazy, complain or resist because they feel heard and 'part of something larger'. If the hiring process is stringent and the conversation ongoing those types of people will likely never be hired. Or if they are, they will be ejected from the company fairly quickly. In this respect a strong culture is *self-regulating*. The employees who embody the cultural values ensure that acceptance is strictly regulated and membership contingent upon adherence to those values.

Takeaways:

- Your culture will create your company. Any value you attain will result from your people and their interactions, which equals your culture.
- If you don't consciously form a culture, you will have to 'take whatever you get', so
- Start talking about culture on day 1. Make the conversation conscious and intentional.
- Establish your values and intentions clearly and openly.
- Ensure those values translate at all levels of hiring.

- Ask the hard questions…be transparent.
- Continue the conversation throughout the life of the company. Be diligent.
- When the company gets big enough, hire someone to head this department.
- Do off-sites and regular company gatherings…from day 1.

Case 1: Faking it

As the CEO of a growing, 7-year-old tech company, Sean thought he knew his culture. After all, he had worked with most of these people from the very first day...and yet he could not believe what he was reading. Sean had been working with investment bankers to take the company public and so had 'Googled' his company to gauge how the market would perceive his firm. During his search Sean found an on-line posting site where employees could vent about their employers. What he saw made him feel sick to his stomach.

One post about his company declared that 'the leadership team is clueless', and that 'the CEO is completely out of touch and lies to his employees.' Another mentioned 'the cruelty of the managers.' A third employee ranted that 'this company is going nowhere' and that 'this business is dying every day.' Sean was at first stunned, and then angry. How could these people turn on him like this? The worst post was the one that ranted 'the culture at this company is TOXIC!' There were only 60 people in the entire company! He knew every person by name!

Sean knew he had to do something, because the bankers and investors would undoubtedly find these postings. In response, he had his HR department 'game' the reviews by posting positive or neutral comments from fictional employees. This strategy backfired as the employees saw through the ruse and publicly accused him of manipulation and deceit. In the end, Sean was forced to spend hundreds of hours explaining to potential investors why these reviews were not accurate and why the company was indeed in a successful position. To date the IPO is still in limbo.

Case 2: A Lasting Influence

From day 1, co-founders Jennifer, Bob and Martin were concerned about the culture of the company they were building (ABC Corp). They knew that everything they accomplished was going to come from the people they were leading, and so they determined at the outset to make culture a priority. In some of their very first meetings they talked about values and the work environment they wanted to create. They came up with core 'founding principles' that included transparency, communication, respect and service. With each new employee they talked about these principles and expanded the definitions to include the new-hire's perspective. As the company grew, the CEO (Jennifer) asked Martin to be the 'cultural leader' who would hold regular off-sites to discuss adaptations, modifications and adherence to the values and processes.

After 5 years of successful operations the company was purchased by a much larger multinational organization. Upon speaking with the employees of ABC Corp, one of the acquirer's executives commented to Jennifer that he 'had never seen a company culture so cohesive and effective.' The executive was so impressed that he asked the founders to help the larger company (a very well known firm with a huge market cap) create a similar culture. 'I was stunned,' Jennifer recounted. 'All we did was focus on values, and we ended up not only making gobs of money but also were able to make a difference in thousands of lives after the acquisition.' The CFO commented later that 'ABC Corp was the best company I have ever worked for. It was not only an effective team, but people were genuinely happy. I did not realize until later that not every company operates like this…it was truly remarkable!'

LESSON 5: DON'T RIDE THE ROLLER COASTER

Life has ups and downs. One day you feel like you are on top of the world, while another day will present you with obstacles that test your patience and faith. Anyone who has taken a moment to reflect knows that living involves a mix of pleasure and pain, triumph and failure, highs and lows. I tend to think of life as a wonderful exploration of the self…if I am willing to stand above the fray and see my experiences as a grand learning experience.

I have always had an optimistic view of life and its possibilities. I have also, however, been sorely tested in my time as an entrepreneur. A quote I read the other day said that 'if you want to grow on every level…physically, emotionally, mentally and spiritually…then start a company'. I have found this to be true because I have been 'through the ringer' in so many situations. There have been days when I thought I was going to be the next Richard Branson or Bill Gates…followed by days when I wasn't sure if I was going to be able to pay the rent. The extremes of experience have driven me almost mad with uncertainty.

Running a company is like caring for a baby. A big, fat, bawling, endlessly hungry, unbelievably petulant, pain-in-the ass baby. Some days you are so proud your heart feels like it is going to burst. You have created something that employs people, provides valuable services and gives you a second family. Through your company you leave an impression on the world. Your love is made visible. On the other hand, you also have a dependent. Your company is, in legal terms, a separate entity that requires care and feeding. When it needs you it is not rational or compromising. If you want to keep it alive you must sometimes sacrifice yourself and your desires on its behalf. You are *responsible*, and this can create stress in even the most centered of people.

When you create your company you are creating an extension of yourself. You take on responsibilities that magnify whatever you experience in life. Pleasures and irritations get bigger and more intense. If you like projects and love to create, then you will love the magnified feelings you get when you watch your team build something truly useful. If you hate taxes, on the other hand, then you will be tested as you deal with governmental complexity like never before. Everything you do as an entrepreneur will 'push your buttons' in both a positive and negative way, especially as it relates to money.

Being attached to making money can bring some of the most

stressful tests of all. Certainly a company can deliver you wealth and prosperity, but if you see that as an end in itself you will likely be in for a wild ride. *Everything* you do will cost more than you think, and the income you hope for will most likely fall short at some point. Even your most conservative estimates will sometimes seem unattainable. You will be tempted to think 'If I can only get through the first year, then I will know if I am going to be successful'. You won't. Every day will bring more uncertainty, even when you are highly profitable. One day you can be making gobs of money and the next day lose your largest client and be hit with an enormous tax bill. For an entrepreneur being attached to money is like trying to hug a cloud...you can grasp and grasp but will never be truly certain about what you have.

If life is a roller coaster, then starting a company is like choosing to ride the wildest, craziest roller coaster you can possibly imagine. And it can be dangerous to your health if you are not careful.

The key to staying sane and healthy when building a company is to avoid riding the roller coaster in the first place. You must be able to stand above the daily fray and look at the craziness with a calm, long-term perspective. The truth is that no one day-to-day result is going to make or break your company or your life. Success is a series of on-going creative actions, not one event. If you lose that deal, then you must take a deep breath and soldier on. If you win a huge contract, then you must smile and soldier on. Take everything in stride. You can celebrate, to be sure, but you must do so in a way that celebrates your *efforts*, not your *outcomes*. In this way you celebrate your persistence and dedication rather than the external world's rewards. If you are attached to rewards (i.e. making money) then every loss will be extremely painful. However if you see your efforts as a grand life adventure then you will always be happy to do the work, regardless of what outcomes it creates.

I learned this the hard way. I have had many needlessly sleepless nights. At one point I even ended up in the emergency room with stress related heart irregularities. When you cease to love what you do and seek only the external reward, then you are going to be yanked to and fro by the randomness of external events. In trying to control the uncontrollable you experience stress, and this can literally kill you (and your business). If you want to thrive you must see yourself and your work as an ongoing act of love and be completely detached from the outcomes. If you can manage this, then you will experience the joy of pure creation.

One way to think about this is what Jim Collins, in his book <u>Built to Last</u>, refers to as 'clock building versus time telling'. If you are telling time you are focused only on results, and these results will never be consistent. You are trying to attach to something that is ever changing. If you are focused on clock building, on the other hand, you are seeking to build a system that produces results every day. The better the system you create, the better the results. Even more importantly, the more sound your system, the better it can survive without you. This is how you create something that not only *produces* but also *thrives*. When you create a powerful system the pressure is transferred from you to the operation, thus relieving any stress and over-responsibility. Living a fun and creative life allows you to focus your energy on building rather than internal destruction.

An example of 'time-telling' is the 'exit strategy'. When an entrepreneur starts a company with an exit strategy in mind (s)he is essentially saying 'I am in this temporarily, and mainly for the money'. It is virtually impossible to create something great if you are only doing it to get rich as quickly as possible. For this reason I encourage my client entrepreneurs to think big, to create a vision of greatness that inspires and attracts. When the vision of the future is powerful and positive – when you are building a 'clock' - then investors, employees and partners will be much more likely to want to help. If the vision is merely to 'exit', to 'tell time', then everyone involved is going to hedge their bets.

I know first hand how challenging it can be to pull yourself out of the weeds and focus on long term value creation. At times it can seem virtually impossible. When the board or investors or customers (or all three) are 'riding your ass'; when cash flow is tight; when you are going home to a significant other who is angry about not seeing you in daylight for 5 days; when your body is exhausted and sick, it may seem like a luxury to think long term. But this is precisely what you have to do. You must find a way to both accept what is happening while at the same time remaining optimistic and focused on the long-term vision. This is the way to survive the crucible of start-up life.

Remember, you can do anything if you focus on where you are going, maintain a positive attitude, stay open to learning, and take small actions every day. Success is not a *miracle*...it is a *process*!

Key Takeaways:

- Focus on creating a great organization.
- Let go of day-to-day results.
- See every day as an opportunity to serve.
- Take breaks!
- Allow yourself to dream of the greater vision, and communicate that vision often.
- Put every event in perspective. It is only one moment in a long life!
- Express gratitude for what you have.
- Do what you can do today, then let go of expectations.
- Treat everything as a learning experience.

Case 1: Wild Ride

This example comes from my own experience.

In 2003 I was 3 years into a technical startup based in Los Angeles. The company started 2000 when the main two founders asked me to participate as a co-founder and CTO. Since inception we had raised over $30 million, survived the 'internet crash' of 2001, changed business models entirely, built one of the world's largest private computer networks, moved offices 4 times, and relocated from Boston to LA. During one trip to New York I had a personal 'close call' on September 11, 2001. I was waiting for a meeting downtown when we heard that planes had crashed into the World Trade Center. For the next two days I was stranded in midtown New York watching people streaming northward away from the chaos. I knew 4 people who had perished either on the planes or in the buildings.

Being older than my partners, I was feeling the pressure of the long hours and endless worry. The market was not producing as much revenue as we had hoped and the burn rate was unsustainable. Investors were calling to express their concerns. Board members were supportive but insistent. The team was frustrated and concerned about our future. I felt like I could not get out from under the relentless pressure of meeting our quarterly expectations. My response was to drink more coffee, worry more, and beat myself up on a daily basis. One day I came into work and got a nasty call from a customer, after which I found myself sitting on the floor of my office having a panic attack. That night I went to the emergency room with an irregular heartbeat and shortness of breath.

All of this was, of course, stress related and highly unnecessary. The company ended up doing fine and was sold in 2005. The investors and founders made money. Looking back, I am surprised at how seriously I took everything. My worry was a colossal waste of energy! Today I know to take everything in stride and let go of any day-to-day bumps. I trust that everything will turn out great, and this has made a huge difference in my ability to create and to sustain my own productivity.

Case 2: Laughing Through Worry

Dana loves to laugh. She finds humor everything, even the bad stuff. And having started an apparel retail store right before the 'great recession' of 2007, she had a lot to laugh about. Almost immediately after starting the store the economy tanked and she had no idea if her small store was going to survive. One month she was selling $5,000 per day, and the next she barely cleared $1,000. Although she tried to keep all of her employees, she simply could not afford the payroll and had to lay off half of her staff and double the hours for the rest (including her). "Don't get me wrong," she recalled in 2014, "I was scared stiff. Every day was touch and go. But I still believed that we offered wonderful product and amazing service. So I just figured out a way to keep going."

Over the next five years Dana struggled to carve out a living while the economy slowly – very slowly – improved. She was able to eventually pay down her debt, pay off her condo, and keep a small crew of staff employed…with health insurance. "You just have to keep your sense of humor, look at the long term, and not take anything too seriously. I found that if I could just focus on what I could do today to make things better I could let go of the worry for a while. I also found a great deal of meaning in my second family, my employees. Their dedication and wiliness to help was so inspiring it still brings me to tears."

As of today Dana's business has returned to profitability and is beginning to grow. Most importantly, she has been able to pay herself for the first time in 3 years. "I have learned to simply laugh my way through the difficult times" she shrugs. "There is nothing in business worth ruining my life for. Worrying simply makes no sense to me now. I can only do what I can do. So I try every day to be thankful for life, to focus on creating value, and to be kind to everyone I know. And so far it seems to be working!"

LESSON 6: BELIEVE IN POTENTIAL, AND EMPOWER YOUR PEOPLE

Every human being, every thought, and every object has creative potential. As an entrepreneur it is your job to find and release that potential. Traditional management focuses on doubts. If you were trained in a large corporation you likely experienced micromanagement, negative reinforcement and punishment for risk-taking. These methods all *deny* potential. You must look for the creative possibility in all people, situations and ideas in order to unlock the power of your enterprise.

Finding and releasing potential is easy, but it requires a shift of thinking. It is very easy to look for what is wrong, what needs to be done, or what is missing. If you are a problem solver like me, then you can easily see the ten things that are missing from every situation. You can quickly identify what someone is doing wrong, how they might improve, and all the things that need to be done to make a situation 'better.' Do not fool yourself, however. This type of 'critical thinking', while sometimes helpful, does nothing to inspire and release the deeper potential in the world. Potential is only released when you open your mind to new paradigms and possibilities.

In stepping into the world of possibility, you must first wrap your head around the idea that within literally every-thing lies hidden potential…especially people. Every problem has a hidden opportunity. Every object has another use. Every situation can be re-interpreted in a positive way. *Every person has a gift waiting to be given.* When you embrace these ideas you shift your mind away from limitation and toward creation.

As an entrepreneur you are in the business of creating something from nothing. It is your job to see what, to date, has not been seen. In order to do this it is incumbent upon you to let go of anything old and embrace the idea that you may not yet see what is possible. This is the essence of creativity…the ability to see the 'unmanifest' and help it come into being. You can develop the ability to conjure thoughts that give form to the formless, and bring the hitherto unknown into reality. Doing this requires discipline. You must be able to see the positive in everything and everyone, and this is not easy in a society that values a critical approach.

In school you learned not to look for what you got right, but for how many answers you missed. Teachers, coaches and parents tell you to 'get back into line', 'go to your seat', 'be quiet and cooperative.' Out of the box thinking is discouraged in order to make you manageable.

In turn you learned to identify all the things that bring you pain, all of the ways you are wrong and unworthy of love. This you called 'prudence' because it gave you a sense of safety. You learned what *not* to do in order to pass for an acceptable human being.

Then you learned how to think in a structured way. Science, grammar, mathematics and sports all gave you structures that allowed you to safely navigate the world of thought and action. You learned to find the so-called 'right' and 'wrong' answers, and so were able to get good grades, get a job and find the right type of spouse. Yet in the process you lost some of your ability to think in an unstructured way. Your inner 'creative child' was pushed aside as too hopeful, too naïve, too simple.

In starting a company you must bring back your creative self and let go of structure. You must see past all the limitations and rules and open yourself to the unknown. Only then can you see the infinite potential that exists before your very eyes.

Let's start with an object…the simplest form of being. Right now, take off your shoe and place it on your desk. This object seems to have a number of uses, yet might seem limited in its potential. As you examine your shoe you can see that it can protect your foot, of course, but also may act as a doorstop, paper holder, glove (if you can do a handstand), and a few other things. Eventually you will run out of things that you think your shoe can do. When this happens, try one simple exercise: Shift your perspective. Sit on the floor. Invert the shoe. Change *anything* about your position and see what happens.

You will likely find that a few more potential uses for this object spring to mind. This is how you unleash potential.

If a situation seems intractable, ask yourself how you can look at it in another way. Where is the opportunity? What can you learn? Even the most difficult times can offer incredible breakthroughs. Shift your position, look for the potential! Napoleon Hill once said "Every adversity, every failure, every heartache carries with it the seed of an equal or greater benefit." You must find this benefit.

Nowhere is this idea more important than in managing and leading people. Every human being, no matter how 'simple' or 'mean' or 'useless', has a gift inside. Everyone has something to offer. In order to lead people to greatness you must first acknowledge this basic truth. When you deeply believe in the potential of others you can then see and encourage that potential. You can *inspire* others to greatness. This does not mean you have to be easy on them. In fact, you can be very, very hard on their performance. Yet underneath your demands lies your belief that they can do anything…and you expect them to live to their highest potential.

When you look at the people around your enterprise…be it vendors, employees, partners or customers…ask yourself: What are the gifts they can offer? How can you acknowledge and encourage those gifts? When you are tempted to criticize or complain, think of the things a person *can* do well and talk about those. Notice successes, accomplishments, possibilities. Encourage others to live into their highest selves. Teach them what you know, then let them make mistakes. Support their efforts to grow. Find the right opportunities and let them go after them. Coach where it is useful, but don't necessarily be prescriptive. Individuals need to own their own thoughts and ways of solving problems. The faster they grow, the more they can take on and open areas for YOU to grow.

If you can develop your ability to see the potential in everything and everyone, then you will graduate to the highest form of leadership. You will become inspirational and powerful. People will want to work for you and with you. Vendors will see you as a thought leader. Customers will revere your optimism. Employees will look to you for guidance and education. You will be able to offer difficult feedback to almost anyone because they will know and trust your underlying motivations. People will know you as a thoughtful person who believes in hope and possibility. They will have faith in you.

The entire universe is one of potential. Everything in your physical world started billions of years ago as an incredibly dense point of light, a seed, a singularity. Indeed, every atom carries within it the possibility of becoming something greater. Your job, as an entrepreneur, is to look at the world through the lens of possibility and open yourself to a new and larger manifestation of the universe. This is not simply ethereal jabber! It is real and we have seen it work!

Key Takeaways:

- Critical thinking is helpful, but look for the possibility *first*.
- Praise what is good about another person. Notice potential.

- Give feedback only when you are sure that a person knows your belief in them and their potential.
- Look for the opportunity in every difficult situation.
- Look for and create opportunities for others to grow.
- Be supportive and coach where needed, but don't always be prescriptive.
- Recognize that every thought and idea contains within it a kernel of truth. Be open to all truths.
- Speak to people's higher nature and abilities. Inspire rather than criticize.
- Talk more about *why* you are doing what you are doing, and less about what.
- When stuck, shift your perspective. Go for a walk. Open yourself to new ways of being. Allow your natural creativity to come forward.

Case 1: The Toxic Boss

Mark was the founder of a management consultancy. He was smart, driven, and well-connected. He was also arrogant, controlling and, to his employees, just plain mean. "Mark would call me into his office and have me sit in a chair that was too low for his desk," a former consultant recalled. "He would try to humiliate me in every way possible. He told me he did not believe in me and that I was merely a cog in his overall scheme to make money. I don't know why I worked for him. It seemed he had me in some sort of trance." Another consultant remembered "…the time when Mark came into my office, sat down at my desk, and then smiled as he took all my pens and pencils and put them in his pocket. He looked at me and said 'because I can'." Each of these employees quit soon after, and to this day remember Mark as one of the worst bosses they have ever had.

Ultimately Mark was forced out of his own company when the firm's revenues dropped significantly and the new investors demanded he relinquish leadership. "I actually learned a lot from Mark," a former consultant recalled. "I learned that caring about people and believing in them is not an option, it is a requirement. When I work with people – clients, employees, partners, whatever – I now think 'what would Mark do?' in order to remind myself to do the opposite. In the end, fear just doesn't work…positive support is the only thing that keeps people inspired, interested and loyal." Today, Mark spends his days showing off the money he made from the buyout and trying to regain the respect of the people around him. Nobody is buying.

Case 2: Finding a Home

Brendan is one of those guys you love to love. He is amiable, collegial and a lot of fun to be around. "I still love Brendan," recalled a former colleague. "He is just such a good guy!" To his bosses, however, Brendan was a bit of a scatterbrain. "The guy just could not organize anything to save his life," remembers a former manager. "He missed meetings, forgot action items, and dropped important tasks. More than once we thought about letting him go."

Terry, Brendan's current manager, had a different take: "I saw immense potential in Brendan's likability. He generated such good will that I thought I might be able to harness that to our benefit." After Terry took over, his first move was to put Brendan in business development. "I took a leap of faith and decided to let go of any expectations," Terry recalled later. "I told Brendan that I wanted him to do what he does best: go out and make friends." True to form, Brendan was disorganized and frustrating to work with. It took him over 6 months to get up to speed, and his progress reports were dismal at best. Just as Terry began to question his decision, however, something happened.

In Terry's words: "Brendan came to me about 6 months in and said he had become close with someone at a potential client. This new friend had recently been promoted to a position of influence regarding our product and wanted to work with Brendan. Fast forward to today...this person is now our largest customer and accounts for 30% of our total revenue. He is also so loyal to Brendan that I don't think they would ever leave us. Sure, Brendan is still a pain in the ass to work with but I will never, ever again doubt his potential to make a difference. Now when I hear someone complain about an employee, my first thought is, 'how can I put them in a place where they can thrive?' To be a good leader you absolutely must look for the potential in those around you."

LESSON 7: INVESTORS ARE EVERYWHERE, BUT CHOOSE CAREFULLY

When starting a company, it is a great temptation to take the first money that comes along. In my first startup I remember feeling so relieved that someone was willing to fund our computer purchases that I considered giving up a third of the company for $50,000 of investment capital. Luckily, I realized that this was an absurd proposition and that the 'investor' - a cash flush friend who wanted to ride on my coattails – was not going to be able to provide anything except money and a brief sense of consolation.

Money is everywhere. If you think about it, money is very much like energy in that it flows around us all the time. They key to getting money is, like energy, finding a way to tap into the flow. Yet so many of us have a 'lack mentality' when it comes to money that we view it as hard to get, hard to keep, and only for the fortunate few. This belief system keeps us from tapping into an infinite source of capital that can grow virtually anything we decide to create.

If you are looking for money you must first address any notions of 'lack' that you may be holding. Do you see money as hard to get? Did you grow up hearing that 'money does not grow on trees'? Does your family view rich people as 'the lucky few'? Look back on your history. What is your relationship to money, and how has it impacted your life? If you are living month to month and stress about bills, then you have a mentality of lack. Your notions about money have created your life. If you see money as easy to get, however, and have truly never worried about it, then you have a mentality of abundance that will allow you a relaxed countenance as you seek investors.

Creating a mentality of abundance is critical because it allows you to pitch with a more confident feeling inside. You see money as an opportunity rather than a problem. If you approach an investor with a lack mentality it will come across as begging. If you approach someone with an abundance mentality it will look like confidence. Abundance is attractive, while lack is repellent. People with money know this because *this is how they made money themselves.* Wealthy people got where they are by being open to the flow of abundance in the world, and you must do the same.

Developing an abundance mentality requires that you see the universe as infinitely full. Do you think, for instance, that $1,000,000,000 (1 *billion* dollars) is a lot of money? If you do, consider the size and scale of the universe. One estimate has the universe as containing approximately 10,000,000,000,000,000,000,000,000 (10 yoctillion) *stars.* And our sun alone, according to NASA, puts out 5,000,000,000,000,000,000,000,000 horsepower *per second*…enough energy to melt a bridge of ice 2 miles wide, 1 mile thick, and extending the entire way from the earth to the sun. Again, this is *per second*. Considering the number of stars, the energy in the universe is absolutely staggering (and this does not include all the 'dark energy' we are just now learning to estimate). The point is that money, which is essentially stored energy, is everywhere, nearly infinite, and merely needs to be redirected into your pocket!

How, then, do you create a mentality of abundance? It is actually quite simple, but requires discipline and a desire to change your current state. As I said above, you must first identify your limiting beliefs about money. Do you hold any negative views about rich or successful people? If you do, then you must acknowledge and release those beliefs by doing the *opposite*. For example, if you look at wealthy people with scorn, derision or envy, then you will need to embrace those very people. Get to know them. Admire them. Read about their successes. Once you embrace *others'* successes then you will open yourself to your own.

Second, you will need to picture your life as one of possibility and abundance. You must *see* your life before you can make the image real. Visualization is a great way to do this. Wake up each morning with an image of prosperity in your head. See the life you want to lead. Picture the profitable business and the full bank accounts. Imagine the infinite flow of the universe streaming into your pocket.

Expand your view of what life has to offer. Visualizing an expansive, abundant future will open you to receiving that truth.

Third, begin to act as if you already had money. Be generous. Inspire others with stories of hope. Associate with people who have wealth-oriented beliefs. Become unswerving in your belief that everything is possible and available. Speak about *when* you will have your money, not *if*. Move throughout your day with actions that support an abundant mindset. As you do this you may see yourself being pulled backwards toward a mentality of lack…do not waver! Searching for cheap gas or the best coupons wastes your precious time! Focus on actions that put you in the flow of wealth in the world. Be disciplined in your approach!

Once you have shifted your mind from lack to abundance, then you can open yourself to investors. People with money can instantly recognize those who have 'cracked the code', and those who are living in fear and lack. Like electricity, money only flows when the conduit is open between the poles. So when you speak to an investor you must relate to their level of thinking. To you $1,000,000 may seem like a lot. To some investors it is not worth considering. Sometimes it is actually easier to get $10,000,000 than it is to get $1,000,000. Everything is relative and dependent on your perspective.

So when talking to an investor, think big, talk big, and assume that you will eventually get your funds. Not everyone will invest, *but some people will*. Let this knowledge make you confident and persistent in your approach. Speak about *when* you will get your money, and don't hesitate to ask for what you need to be successful. Paint a picture of what you are going to do to make your investors even *more wealthy*. When you speak from a place of extreme confidence people will stop for a moment and think 'what if he/she is right?' Everyone wants to be associated with a winner...so act like one!

Now that you have inspired people to pour money into your venture, you will need to do the unthinkable: Reject some of them. Yes, money is a commodity, but it is also energetically tied to human beings. The people who own the money can be helpful, hurtful or neutral. You want to attract money that is helpful. In the investor world, this is called 'smart money'. Smart money comes from people who know your industry, have contacts, are experienced in starting companies, or are generally supportive of your efforts. Smart money can introduce you to potential customers and investors. Smart money is on your side.

On the other side, 'dumb money' can be useless or, at worst, hurtful. Your former college roommate who struck it big in the lottery is dumb money. I am not saying that this person is dumb, only that the money is only helpful to its numerical value. Friends and family are the same...they can only put in cash and then stand on the sidelines. No matter how much your friends like you, they can't help you much beyond what they invest. This money is not bad, per se, but you want to be careful how much of it you use. In the beginning it may be all you can get, so you can take it without worry. In later rounds, however, 'smart money' investors will be looking to see who has invested in your company. If you have chosen mainly 'dumb money' over a long period of time then they will doubt whether your idea has market validity. Smart investors are always looking to see the other 'smart' investors that have signed on to your plan.

Even smart investors, however, can be hurtful. It is important to find people you like and who will be supportive of your efforts. If you find someone who is 'plugged in' in the industry but hassles you and beats you up at every turn, then they are not *smart for you*. You want an investor that meets at least some of the following criteria:

- Trustworthy
- Understands the industry
- You like
- Has contacts with investors, partners and clients
- Shares your vision for the company
- Is prepared to be patient with you
- Is known in the investor world (e.g. a good brand name)

I understand it may be hard to find a firm or person who meets all of these criteria. The point is to look carefully at who you are asking to join your business. An investor is a *partner*, and you should treat them with almost the same concern as I mention in the previous chapter on partnership. Your investors will be with you for a long time, so make sure you choose people who make you feel good about yourself and your business.

Even with good choices, however, you may still encounter investors who act in a non-team-oriented way. Investors can, for example, band together to try to vote you out. If you have a number of VC's in your investor pool they may contact one another and join their votes to get their way. Or they may try to co-opt you in order to get you to sell out the other shareholders through the 'cram-down' process (in which more shares are sold to dilute existing shares). There are many ways for investors to manipulate and turn on you or other investors, so you have to be very careful how not only you choose your partners but also how you manage them. Remember, you are swimming with sharks! Smart money can also be crafty money!

One of the ways to keep smart money in check is to be very aware of your capitalization table, or 'cap table'. A cap table is a list of all the shareholders and the percentage of stock they own. Every time you sell more stock (get investors) your cap table changes. As you sell stock you are always looking to keep your share of ownership the highest it can be…ideally over 51%. When you own 51% of your company you are in control, and an investor cannot easily manipulate you. A VC will always be looking to maximize their ownership stake, and thereby get more and more control of your company. If you let your ownership slide below 51%, then you lose control and the other investors can vote you out. Because of this you must constantly monitor the ownership percentages such that you maintain control for as long as possible.

There is much more to learn about investors and the investment world, and I recommend that you embark on this journey with care. Learn as much as possible, question all motives, and always seek to keep voting control. Everything else will take care of itself.

Key Takeaways:

- Money is everywhere. It is abundant and available.
- Create a mindset of abundance *before* seeking funds.
- Find and release any 'lack' stories in your psyche.
- Form a cap table for your company and always monitor control.
- Use 'dumb money' in the beginning, but not past the initial investors.
- Seek the smartest money whenever possible. Look for a strong brand.
- Make sure you trust your investors…and yet still monitor them.
- Treat an investor like a potential partner. Be picky.

For more information about investment and investors, read <u>Fund Your Dreams: Proven Tools for Pitching Investors</u> *by K.C. Hildreth.*

Case 1: The Price of Money

Bob scanned the Wall Street Journal article and swallowed hard. "Why now?" he asked himself in frustration. His company, a small tech startup, was in the middle of a major fund-raising round and one of his investors was about to blow up the entire process. Bob suspected that Andy had skeletons in his closet, but he had no idea to what extent.

Unknown to Bob, five years prior Andy Brown had been suspected of numerous SEC violations and was now living on a private island off the coast of Canada in order to avoid US law enforcement. When Andy called saying he wanted to invest $5 million in his company, Bob, being elated at his good fortune and unaware of Andy's situation, was very interested. "I could not believe our good luck," Bob explained later. "This guy seemed to be an angel! He was so excited to invest and to be a part of our company. What I did not know was that he was looking for a place to hide his money…and we were that place!"

Due to his excitement, Bob ended up taking $3 million without much due diligence. Only later did he find out the extent of Andy's issues, and by then he could not do anything about it. "In the middle of our $30 million second round, we found out in the WSJ that Andy was being extradited to NY to stand trial," Bob recalled. "I had to call each potential investor and explain the situation. Not only that, Andy had become part of our investor PowerPoint deck! It killed me every time I mentioned his name!" Fortunately Bob was able to close the round in spite of having Andy as an investor. "I will never again take money from an investor without adequate research," Bob said. "To this day I still worry what issues his presence in our business will create."

Case 2: The Loyal Investor

The team was exhausted and demoralized. Three months prior the stock market had crashed and most of their company's competitors were either out of business or fading fast. The company had plenty of cash, but also a very high burn rate and virtually no income...for the foreseeable future. Investors were, as Cheryl, the former CEO, put it, 'freaking out'. "We had investors calling us every single day for weeks," Cheryl remembered. "Yelling, cursing, second guessing our decisions, you name it. Sometimes they would even go around our backs and call our employees directly! I would catch my head of engineering on the phone being grilled by an investor about bug fixes and perceived issues! It was incredibly stressful to manage and control investors with millions of dollars on the line. They were stressed, we were stressed, and, honestly, we couldn't work with them bugging us."

The team was reaching a breaking point until one day when two minority investors showed up at the office. Tom and Steven were partners in a firm that had invested $1 million, and they wanted to check in on the team. Rather than berate anyone, however, they asked to speak to the entire company. Cheryl recounts what happened: "They thanked everyone for all the hard work...and not in a perfunctory way. They talked about how grateful they were to have people working so hard on behalf of their investment. Individuals were called out for special attention and positive messages. Then they told us they knew how hard it was to start a company, and how much dedication it took to succeed in a down market. They encouraged us to keep our spirits up and that greatness required perseverance. In closing, both Tom and Steven said that they were professionally and personally behind us 100% and that they cared about our well-being. It still brings tears to my eyes to think about this. Their visit gave us a boost that kept us going and, eventually, helped make us successful."

In the end Cheryl's company was one of the only industry players to make it through the tech crash of 2001. It was eventually purchased for an eight-figure sum, and all of the investors generated a return.

LESSON 8: EXECUTION IS EVERYTHING (NOT YOUR IDEA)

I cannot even count how many times a new entrepreneur has come to me and said "I have this great idea, but I need you to sign an NDA before I tell you." This always gives me a chuckle because I know that there are very, very, very few people who have the time, energy, money, connections and knowledge to start and run a company. The truth is that your idea will be about 5% of your success, so stop worrying about who may or may not steal your brilliant thought. Plus, it has been shown that great ideas never happen one at a time. The likelihood is very high that multiple others have had your thought…so get past your own brilliance and move on to what *is* important: *execution*.

First, however, I must caveat that there are some industries and situations where theft is rampant, and therefore I do recommend caution in the following situations. First is the entertainment industry. Movie and television concepts can be pitched by anyone anywhere, so you want to hold your thoughts to yourself until you get some protection. Second, certain highly technical, specialized and competitive fields like silicon chip manufacture or, believe it or not, food product industries (because recipes are so easy to steal) require care. And in the fast developing world of mobile and tech, simple ideas can be incredibly valuable and quick to market. Last, any industry that is based on proprietary information such as stock trading, banking or information sales must protect ideas because they are easy to transfer.

Other than these situations, don't spend too much time worrying about your idea. Creating a new product, industry or a way of selling products is *really hard*, and it takes a special person to make it happen. One of the greatest mistakes you can make is to think that your idea is so brilliant and so easy that you can make millions with the snap of a finger. If you think this then you have no idea what you are in for. Creating a plan, raising money, hiring the right people, developing your product, finding customers, re-developing your product when it is not right for the market, firing the wrong people, re-hiring others, fending off competitors, keeping costs low, managing cash…THAT is the 95% you need to worry about.

Brilliant execution is the key to any enterprise, and it takes five key ingredients. First, you must have a plan. Many entrepreneurs think they can get along without planning, and this is a mistake. Planning forces you to think about all the details *before* you hit the market. The plan itself is obsolete from the day you finish it, yet it is an indispensable starting point. Without a plan you will inevitably miss something, and people will see your uncertainty…especially investors.

Second, you need to be thorough and pay attention to details. There are literally hundreds, sometimes thousands, of things to think about when you are creating an enterprise. Your plan will help you identify your 'to-do's', but you also must manage your own activity to keep track of what you have done, what you are working on, and what you still need to do. Some of the worst blow-ups I have seen in the start-up world (especially tech startups) have come because the founders could not follow through on the myriad of tasks that are shown in the plan. Instead, the founders assume that everyone else is doing the detail work, and in the end nobody knows what is happening at the ground level.

Third, you must be willing to take risks…to your ego more than anything else. Startups are inherently risky, so you would think that all entrepreneurs are willing to do the 'hard things' to make themselves successful. Not so. I have found that many startups fail simply because the founders are afraid to step out at key points. For some it may be in calling customers or pitching lower level executives, and for others it shows up in pitching investors. One very common ego-related issue is the reluctance to release a product before it is 'perfect'. Resistance and fear can pull even the most daring founders back into their shells, so it is important to be vigilant and self-driven. Every day you must be willing to step out of your comfort zone and do the things that you fear. Every day you must risk your ego for the sake of success.

Fourth, and this I cannot emphasize enough, you must have persistence and dedication to the vision of what you are creating. In this world of 'instant gratification', many entrepreneurs give up simply because success is not coming fast enough. The painful truth is that success takes time and energy, and so you must prepare yourself to push through until the end. You will encounter technical hurdles, fears, resistances, boredom, frustration, rejection, failures and blow-ups. Individually, every one of these problems can be resolved. Yet are you prepared to push through *all* of them? Are you willing to feel your fears and frustrations and continue anyway? You may say yes now, but I know from experience that when all these things happen at once, or seem to happen over and over for 2 years, it is easy to question your resolve. Are you willing to keep going when every fiber of your being wants to just 'get a job' and move on? Your answer is the key behind executing success!

Last, you need to be able to learn and adapt. Sometimes entrepreneurs find it confusing when I say that they to be both persistent and adaptable. Persistence does not mean *rigidity*. Persistence is the dedication of energy. Adaptability is the willingness to take in new information and modify course if necessary. To adapt does not mean to give up…it simply means to adjust your assumptions and proceed in a slightly new direction. One of the greatest attributes an entrepreneur can have is the ability to learn. If you can absorb information from the people and situations around you, then you can use that information to adjust your plan and increase your odds of success. If you can't learn, you can't grow.

The reason that execution is so difficult for most entrepreneurs is that to do it well you must do *all* of the above steps well. Some people are great at planning, but don't want to take risks. Others love risks but can't plan their way out of a paper bag. Still others are stubbornly persistent and detail oriented, but won't listen to anybody. If any one of these things are missing, then the chances of building a successful business drop markedly. I encourage you to test this for yourself. Find any business that failed and you will likely find one of these 'failures of execution' behind the scenes. As an entrepreneur your job is not so much to do everything perfectly as it is to make sure your execution process is diligent in all areas.

One final note on people. There are very few people in the world who are great at execution. Most everyone will talk a big game, but it takes a special person to see a vision and truly go for it. If you are choosing a partner, employee or vendor, make sure that you evaluate them as to how good they execute on their ideas or projects. Ask about past successes and failures. Notice their response in the face of adversity. Do they quit easily? Did they learn from failures? Are they willing to take risks when it counts? Look for details in their responses. A lack of detail is a red flag that can mean the person really wasn't the one that executed. If you can find someone who answers these questions favorably, you will likely have an 'executor' on your hands. A person like this is worth their weight in gold. A person who cannot execute is dead weight at best, and a success killer at worst.

Key Takeaways:

- Your idea is a small part of your business. Execution is much more important.
- Execution is composed of planning, attention to detail, risk taking, persistence and dedication, and adaptability.
- Practice rapid product iteration. Get your product or service out quickly, test the market, and then re-design if necessary. Perfection is impossible.
- If you can execute, you can make almost anything successful.
- If you cannot execute, your idea is worthless.
- Very few people can execute on an idea or plan. Be picky with whom you choose to work. Look for details on past projects.

Case 1: All Smoke, No Fire

Barry is an idea machine. On any given day he comes up with brilliant concepts and is able to pitch them with aplomb. To the unwary listener, Barry is a brilliant entrepreneur with the 'next big thing' happening all the time. He always has an NDA handy so that nobody will steal his ideas, which many times are actually quite good. There is an energy in Barry that is infectious and exciting!

The problem is that Barry finds it very difficult to do anything.

When I first met Barry I mistakenly believed that he would be a good person to coach as he seemed intelligent, eager, inspirational and driven. I took him on as a pet project, feeling that his ideas were strong enough that I could get him to a successful place fairly quickly. I learned just as quickly, though, that Barry had a block that prevented him from taking effective action. Each time he created a team and tried to build something, he would get lost in his own ideas. His momentum would stall and his team would become demoralized. No matter how promising the idea, Barry would end up back on the street pitching his next great plan.

Barry still struggles with this issue. Right now he is living in a friend's basement, still talking about the next big thing.

Case 2: Masters of Adaptation

It was the year 2000 and the founding team of a tech company was experiencing the crash of the 'tech bubble'. Businesses were going under left and right, and their own business model was under threat. Initially the founders had pictured their startup as a large scale gaming company relying on advertising revenue. This model was common in the pre-crash world and seemed to be the answer to gaining 'eyeballs'. Now, however, the market was changing and the huge game they built was clearly not going to attract enough people to generate a large market cap.

Over the previous 6 months the team had been masters of execution. In record time they built one of the largest privately-owned networks in the world, assembled a crack team of developers, raised $30 million, and created a massive parallel gaming software. They prided themselves on their ability to do things faster than anyone thought possible. Now they were sorely tested, because the model they built was simply not going to work.

TJ, the CEO and main founder, recalled later, "We had to do something quickly. Our cash was running out and we were still paying for this enormous system we had built. We came to the conclusion that we had to switch our business model or we were going to go under like all of our competitors." The team held a weekend of strategy sessions and came up with a plan that completely re-configured the entire business. Within 12 months they had transformed themselves into an entertainment company, relocated to Los Angeles, and built a thriving television technology business.

"It really does not matter what you are doing," TJ says today. "The important thing is to know how to do what you are doing. You have to build, assess, reconfigure and then build again. Nothing stays still. You must aggressively take action and create something, or else your ideas are worthless."

LESSON 9: DEVELOP YOUR PERSISTENCE MUSCLE

There are many quotes and statistics about how, and why, startups fail. Academics talk about cash flow, industry dynamics and funding challenges. Investors talk about lack of leadership, sales results and technical issues. Entrepreneurs refer to stress, overwork, impossible customers and shrinking margins. All these reasons are true, and yet I have found that they all share a common, root cause:

The underlying reason most startups fail is because their founders simply *give up*.

Yes, an entrepreneur can experience debilitating changes in the industry that make it very, very difficult to make money. Or they can face an almost impossible funding environment. Or it can be a lawsuit or unscrupulous partner. Whatever the reason for the struggle, every startup leader faces a fundamental choice: To go on or to stop trying. Everyone has a threshold of pain that determines how far they are willing to go, and in my experience that limit is very low for most people.

The difference between ordinary people and highly successful entrepreneurs is the ability to *persist through the pain.*

Look back on your life. Do you tend to give up easily? Do you surrender when things get tough? Examine your relationships, career challenges and jobs. Be honest with yourself. What is your tendency…to push through or to leave? This soul searching is important because most people tend to believe they will be able to push through when their past says otherwise.

I am an avid hiker. The longer and more challenging the hike the better. Over the years I have hiked with many people, some of whom were 'old hands' while others had never been in the woods. Over the past 40 years I have hiked with these people on some brutally long treks in very inhospitable places. I have seen people, including myself, pushed to the physical breaking point, and learned that people generally do one of two things when hitting this 'break point': They either bear down and push, or they shatter and collapse.

Every person is different. For some people the break point is 2 miles into the hike. For others it comes when the temperature drops to 30 degrees and icy sleet is pelting down. My break point comes with heat…I face my own collapse when it is over 90 degrees and I am going uphill with a heavy pack. No matter how strong you are, there is a point at which your mind starts to wobble, where you feel like you can't, or don't want to, go on. When this happens your brain goes haywire and produces every excuse in the book for quitting. You find yourself saying 'this is not worth it' over and over. This is when you face 'the choice'.

In my hikes I have also learned that I can go much further than I think. Our brains try to convince us that we can't go on, that 'this is it', when in reality we have double, even triple the capacity to continue. If after 10 miles of brutal, uphill slogging my mind is screaming 'I can't take another step', I know now that I have *at least* 10 more miles in me. I have seen people go so far beyond their own limits many times, and know that the human spirit can transcend even the most daunting obstacles. Throughout history people have survived and persisted in ways that boggle the mind. The famous story of Sir Ernest Shackleton gives an example, if you are interested.

My point is that you must prepare yourself for the challenge ahead, because a startup is like a long, hot, difficult, and yet beautiful, hike. You will go up long hills, stumble and fall, slog through swamps, and debate the point of it all. Your endurance and patience will be pushed to the limit, yet if you can persist and push through you will stand triumphant on the mountaintop wondering at what you have accomplished. There is nothing like the feeling of having *succeeded*, and as any successful entrepreneur (or trekker) will tell you it makes all the effort seem worthwhile.

The key to pushing through is to train and strengthen your 'persistence muscle'. You must recognize your own 'break points' and work to push through them at every opportunity. If you know that you get very stressed about money, then seek to develop the ability to live with less. If you get overwhelmed easily with tasks, then learn to organize and delegate to reduce the stress. If you fear uncertainty, then try to desensitize yourself through meditation or faith-based practices. Just like getting in physical shape, you can develop your internal capacity to push through and triumph in the face of challenge.

You may find these practices helpful in your training:

- **Learn to laugh.** One of the best antidotes to a very difficult situation is to laugh out loud. Sometimes the obstacles come so fast and furiously that you can only laugh at the absurdity of it all. On one hike I remember standing in 100-degree heat, with a 50lb pack, on a hill of sand where each step caused me to slide backwards almost as far as I had moved forward. Both my buddy and I were totally delirious with exhaustion. In the middle of the hill we looked at each other and burst out laughing…and that lifted our spirits enough to keep moving. Your *spirit* is what keeps you moving forward! Laughter is food for your spirit!
- **Meditate.** Meditation is more than just a spiritual practice for monks and seekers, it can be a very effective energy management tool as well. The simplest way to describe meditation is that it is a way to step beyond the noise in your mind. When you get stressed your mind gets scared and goes haywire. Thoughts careen around inside your head until your

internal life becomes chaotic and undirected. This is when people quit their quest. When you meditate you focus your mind on a single point, and slowly it quiets down. As your mind goes quiet you will see that you are not in as bad a place as your mind would tell you. Your stress lifts and you are able to continue. Meditation allows you to persist in your pursuit of success.

- **Know when to rest.** When you are starting a company the work is literally endless. If you wanted, you could work 24 hours a day, 7 days a week and still not get it all done. For this reason you MUST plan out your week in such a way that you get significant rest. If you don't plan your breaks, your body and mind WILL force you to do so. I have seen and experienced these 'stress collapses' many times. People start making bad decisions, moods get ornery and efficiency drops. There is a reason every religion recommends a 'sabbath' of some sort each week. You need time to regroup, clear your mind and recharge your batteries. I recommend 1 full day a week completely off (during which you have 3 hours of 'alone time') and 8 uninterrupted hours of sleep each day. And watch caffeine, sugar and alcohol…they can be energy killers.

- **Learn to delegate.** Besides rest, another way to increase your efficiency, your 'leverage', is to become very good at delegating your work. When you delegate, you magnify your effect. Many entrepreneurs have a hard time doing this because they believe that they are the only ones who know enough or care enough to do a good job…and this may be true. But you are only one person, and if you try to do everything you will limit your company and put yourself at risk of burnout. The only answer is to learn to transfer both knowledge and excitement to those who work with you. You must become a teacher and motivator. When you do this well you will find you have people all around you willing to do your work, and this will allow you to persist in your vision.

- **Take the long view.** Many new entrepreneurs have a 'pie-eyed' view of their business. They look at their market and declare 'if we can only get xyz to happen, then everything will be great for us'. In the beginning, I was the same way. Success, money and fame were just around the corner if I could just get one more person to buy my product. I used this belief to motivate myself to achieve, and it worked. The problem was that I became exhausted as each new hurdle I crossed presented more, and higher, obstacles. There was always an 'if only' in front of me, and I got burned out deluding myself. If you are starting a company, you must realize that it is going to take a long time and a lot of hard work. The hurdles will be many. You will never know when your success will pay off, so let go of near term expectations and just try to build a great company. Focus on your long-term vision, and let everything else take care of itself.

- **Keep your mind on the *now*.** If you have a long-term vision in mind, you can let go and keep your thoughts on what you can do *in this moment* to move toward it. One of the ways that people burn themselves out is to worry about the thousand things that need to happen over the next 2 months. Startups move so quickly that you can never know what the next 2 months will look like (let alone 2 days), so stop thinking about it! What do you know you need to do *right now*? What can you do *in this moment* to help move your idea forward? Let go of everything else. Each long trek is just a series of steps. If you can take one step every day then you will find that you go miles over the long term. Like drops of water wearing away a stone, your daily actions will add up over time to move you forward. To persist, do many small things over and over!

- **Stay with what you know.** Another way entrepreneurs burn themselves out, and end up quitting, is by constantly stressing about things they don't know or don't understand. This is understandable because entrepreneurship is all about uncertainty. Everything is unknown because you are trying to create something that does not yet exist! It is ALL a blank slate. Yet it is also true that you DO know some things. You know what you want to create. You know how to learn. You know how to work. You know basic things about what you are doing. If you want to persist you must focus on what you know, and then slowly expand from that base. Do what you know you have to do, and learn about what you don't know. There will always be things that you don't know, so don't waste energy stressing about it. Always ask yourself 'what do I know I can do today?' and then continue forward.

- **Work for fun.** If you listen to most people talk about 'work' you will here them speak of it as difficult, unpleasant and tiring. This notion of work is not only draining, it is untrue. Work does not have to be hard. Work can be creative, exciting, interesting and fun. In order to persist over the long term you must include in your daily work the things that you enjoy doing. When managing others, seek to put them in roles that they enjoy. The idea that work is not fun is an outdated notion that lends to burnout and an inability to persevere over the long term. In order to persist in your venture, and indeed in life itself, you must find the fun, laughter, creativity and joy in what you do.
- **Have faith.** One of the greatest life stressors is what is called 'existential angst', the feeling that things are not going to be OK and that we do not have a place in the world. When we feel like life is not going to turn out, or that we are not safe as we are, then we spend a great deal of time worrying, trying to control, and generally overthinking our existence. Unfortunately, our schools and parents have sometimes reinforced this belief by rewarding us for our fear-based performance. A's are lauded, C's are punished, and so we live in fear that we need to live up to a certain standard in order to be loved. This is not true! Everything you are doing is OK and, in the end, everything will turn out fine. When you

take this view of life you let go of expectations and live more peacefully. I encourage you to find your faith in yourself and in life…be it through God, love, joy, whatever. Faith is the key to longevity and essential to your company's success!

As an entrepreneur your practice is to 'develop your persistence muscle' through these activities. When you are able to laugh, trust, think long term and let go of expectations you free up enormous energy that can be repurposed toward *execution*. Worry, fear and doubt are draining and counterproductive. Negative feelings tend to cloud your judgment, not spur you forward. Have patience with yourself and the arc of your business. Success, in my experience, is not about any one action or event but is instead about faithful and constant execution over a long period of time. When you are able to persist then success becomes not a *possibility* but an *eventuality*.

Key Takeaways:

- Most of the time startups fail because people *give up*.
- Your job is to learn how to push through when things get difficult.
- Persistence is a muscle that can be developed.
- Practice persistence by learning: Laughter, meditation, rest, delegation, long-term thinking, presence in the now, to stay with what you know, to work on what you enjoy, and to have FAITH.
- Fear and doubt are draining and sap your ability to persist.

- Love, trust and faith are energizing and build your ability to persist.
- Learn to persist in the face of obstacles and you can achieve anything.
- When feeling doubt, redouble your commitment to yourself and your craft. Say "I WILL" and move forward.
- You can do anything to which you commit 100% of your mind and body!

Case 1: I'm Done

Ray was shocked to hear his partner say the words. "I quit" was never something he had planned to hear, yet here he stood facing the prospect of going it alone. When Ray chose Atul to be his partner he had had a very specific discussion about the need to push through the hard times, yet Atul seemed to throw all that out the window.

Ray could understand Atul's concerns. The company was bleeding cash, the economy was in free-fall, and an ex-partner had filed a frivolous lawsuit against the company. Investors were increasingly hard to find and the firm was facing the prospect of very lean times. The first indication of trouble came when Atul intimated that he would not let the company's problems affect his home life.

"I was stunned", Ray said of that moment. "Atul and I had talked extensively about how things might get dicey and that we would need to be dedicated over the long term. To hear him so ready to throw in the towel was shocking to say the least. I was furious with him, but it didn't matter." After only 6 months Atul left the company and took a job with a larger firm. The startup he and Ray co-founded continued for another year but eventually closed. Ray reflected later that "some people just can't take the uncertainty and stress of the startup world. They say they are determined, but when things get just a little difficult they give up. I feel bad that I also gave up, but Atul's defection deflated me too much to effectively build the company."

Case 2: Never Quit!

Jim is a dynamo when it comes to business. He never let anyone dissuade him from his vision, even when times get tough. "I refuse to give up", Jim says defiantly. At age 8 he declared that someday he would be a business 'Typhoon', and he is well on his way to doing so. Occasionally people have laughed about Jim's exuberance, but now everyone can see that his persistence has paid off.

To date Jim owns 10 houses, an on-line real estate company, a brewery, and has a career in the medical field. Over time Jim has also tried multi-level marketing schemes, direct sales systems, and various other 'wild' ideas. In Jim's words, "I don't care what anyone thinks, and I don't let go of something I believe in. I know that if I work hard and stay dedicated to what I want, then I can make anything happen." Even when something is not working, Jim simply adapts his idea and continues forward. "Nothing ever 'fails'" Jim says. "People just give up. I don't believe in giving up until I am dead in the ground!"

Case 3: Looking Long Term

Shaun had begun to think there was something wrong with him. He had been working on his 'big idea' for over 10 years and yet nothing was moving forward. He had filed patents, wrote business plans, pitched investors, and spent virtually everything he had trying to make it work. His bank account was near zero and, although he was not a quitter, he was seriously thinking of giving up. "I did not know how much further I could go," Shaun said much later. "I was exhausted, demoralized and starting to wonder if I was completely off my rocker."

Then one day he bumped into a lawyer at a random networking function in his city. This lawyer loved his idea and introduced him to an investor. This investor agreed to fund the concept and introduce Shaun to engineers who could bring the project into reality. "In one night my whole life changed," Shaun recalled. "Everything became real. I saw my product in customers' hands! I still have to pinch myself, all these years later!" Now, Shaun coaches young entrepreneurs for fun. "I tell them to never, ever give up on themselves or their ideas. I know now that persistence is the key to everything, and that eventually your ideas will be seen. 'Dedicate yourself to yourself' is my mantra!"

Shaun is now quite wealthy and his products can be seen in many places around the world.

LESSON 10: LEARN TO LEARN

In earlier chapters I have referenced the need to learn and adapt. This lesson is so important that I believe it deserves its own chapter. Learning is so important that without it a company can quickly stagnate and become irrelevant. Leaders who are unwilling to learn tend to become insular, surrounding themselves with people who agree with their hard and fast positions. When an entrepreneur fails to learn, they fail to open themselves to the possibility that there may be another point of view, and this creates a weakness that can ultimately bring down their business.

For some entrepreneurs, the downside of a strong 'success drive' is that they become blind to all new information. In their quest to implement their strategy they forget that the *market* ultimately determines what will succeed or fail. As much as persistence, drive and dedication matter…and they do…success is also determined by flexibility, openness and willingness to absorb information. Thus success comes only when a leader can use both a direct, hard approach as well as an indirect, softer method. Masculine/feminine, Yin/Yang.

Learning requires humility, and this can be difficult for some leaders. In order to take in new information a person must first admit that they don't know everything. This is hardest for people who consider themselves 'experts' in their fields. In my experience this is most prevalent in academia, engineering and specialized industries. When someone has been studying or working on something for a long time, they tend to view the customer as the ignorant part of the transaction. As entrepreneurs they refuse to recognize that the market is the ultimate decision maker, and that their ideas of what will sell are not necessarily accurate.

We have seen this very often in the software world. A brilliant, highly educated software engineer builds something that he thinks the customer wants. He raises money, builds a prototype, then raises more money and builds a working version. All the while he has forgotten that his design is based on his personal vision of what the customer wants, not what the customer wants in *actuality*. When the product flops in the market the founder is then incensed that the 'stupid customer' does not know quality when they see it. This product myopia is very common in entrepreneurs.

If you want to succeed in a startup then you must, from day 1, resolve yourself to learning…about everything. No matter how smart you are, or how experienced, or how knowledgeable, there is something you do not know. There are people in the world who know more than you about many subjects…you must learn to not only accept that fact, but also *embrace* it. You are surrounded by sources of knowledge and skill, and can learn something new every day if you are willing to open your mind. Here are a few subjects to consider (at a minimum):

- **Sales.** As an entrepreneur, you likely have innate sales skills. Even so, the skill of selling is one that needs to be honed and polished. *If you are not exceptional at selling your product to customers or your company to investors you will find it very difficult to be successful.* Learn everything you can from those who sell for a living! Learning to sell can increase the odds of your success significantly!

- **Leadership/management.** When you hire your first employee you become a manager. When you pitch your company for the first time you assume the role of leader. Do not let your managerial or leadership style develop by accident! Learn to lead from people who have created great organizations. Seek to manage in a positive and professional way. Everyone, no matter how senior, needs to improve their skills in this area.

- **Culture and human dynamics.** A business is a *social enterprise.* Your startup is, first and foremost, a group of human beings trying to create something in the world. In order to best motivate your team you must first understand how they interact and how culture determines success. Study successful organizations. Read about psychology and behavior. Humans are complex creatures…take the time to get to know your species!

- **Operations.** Operational efficiency is the cornerstone of a profitable enterprise. Learning to minimize costs, maximize production, decrease inventory and increase customer retention are all key to ongoing success. As you grow you can learn how to better produce and manage your product, resulting in ever increasing profitability. Learn everything you can from experts in efficient operations.

- **Technology.** Every business has a certain amount of technology embedded in the operations. It may be you are starting a technology company, or you may simply need a web site to support your sales. Either way, it is very helpful to learn about the latest technology in your industry. The technical world is changing constantly. In order to compete you need to know who is using what technical tools, and how they are using them. Always seek to innovate and use the best resources at your disposal!

- **Finance.** After people, business is secondarily about money. Money is the fuel and oil that keeps a company running smoothly. Cash flow problems can kill a company in a matter of weeks…you need to know all the reporting tools used to measure and analyze your company's financial position. Understanding finance can also help you avoid getting 'taken' by savvy investors and bankers. If you are financially smart, you can use the system to your benefit!

- **Marketing.** Good marketing can change your business overnight. One good campaign can literally triple your sales. Further, marketing need not be expensive. There are resources that can teach you how to effectively market your products for little to no cost. Understanding viral loops and social marketing can do wonders for your business or product. Learn how to do this! Viral loops and marketing are a science. Spend the time to understand how they work and how others have been successful.

- **Self-improvement.** You are not a finished product! You are constantly evolving and will continue to do so until you die. Seek to improve yourself, because your business is a reflection of YOU. If you want your business to grow, then you must grow as well. If you want your employees to improve, then you must set the tone yourself. Every day, in every way, seek to grow into a greater person!

In today's information-rich world, you can find sources of knowledge and skills virtually everywhere. There are experts on every topic mentioned above, and the knowledge they possess can be accessed in many ways. Some sources include:

- **Mentors.** There are thousands of people in the world who want to give back. Anyone over the age of 50 has likely considered how they can be of service in the world. There is endless knowledge and experience in those who have gone before you. Find them, and they can help you increase your odds of success (or at least save you from some costly mistakes!).

- **Books.** 130,000,000 books are in print in the world today. Of this number, a large percentage are non-fiction books on every imaginable subject. All you need to do is identify what you want to learn…and dive in! I recommend reading for at least ½ hour every single day. Reading every day not only increases your knowledge, but it also gives you a powerful feeling of growth that will help you keep going when you are feeling unmotivated. Activate your 'book hunger'!

- **Audio.** One of my favorite ways to learn is through audio books and talks. It is easy, efficient (because you can multi-task), and can give you tidbits of information that are useful in your work. I especially like sales tapes. I listen to them in the car on the way to a meeting and almost always get a boost of inspiration before I walk in. If you are trying to raise money make sure you learn to sell! Listen to everyone in the field!

- **Panels.** Every industry has a trade show or annual gathering. And each of these meetings usually has a series of panels on various subjects. The people asked to sit on these panels have deep experience and knowledge in their fields, and so you can learn a lot just by hearing them speak. When attending an event, seek out those who know more than you. Listen to them. Try to get to know them personally and ask questions. Seek out other's knowledge.

- **'Trade rags and websites'.** Every industry also has its pet magazines, periodicals and websites. Some have sophisticated journals (like the AMA), while others have newspaper-like 'rags' that cover the recent industry scuttlebutt (like Entertainment). Subscribe to and read everything published in your industry. Bring yourself up to speed on the latest developments in your field and read about the activities of your competitors. This knowledge will help you immensely with your business and direction. It can help you see different opportunities and trends.

- **Consultants/coaches.** Many people, like myself, eventually leave their industry and form their own consultancies. Their reasons vary widely. For some it is burnout, for others it may be boredom or a desire to have more control over their experience. In my experience, successful older people want a more relaxed life and seek to 'pay forward' what they have learned. No matter what the reason, there are many people out there who have in-depth knowledge about what you are trying to do. Seek them out! Ask their advice! Hire them to help! I have found that my clients make well over 20 times what they have ever spent on my services…a good investment to be sure!

- **Training courses.** One of the smartest things I ever did as a young entrepreneur was to take a course in desktop publishing. As simple as it sounds, this course taught me about publishing, layout, information design, marketing and advertising design. I took this course over 30 years ago, and I *still* use these skills today. Look for courses that will give you any 'edge' in your field. Go to your local college and get a course brochure. Sign up for anything free. Put yourself through your own university!

- **Studies**. Consultancies, universities and trade associations publish studies about every imaginable aspect of your industry. Find who is publishing anything about your business and seek relevant studies. This is especially important as you write your business plan, because any good plan includes information on market size, consumer trends, investment patterns, product research and technical developments. All of this information has been published in a study somewhere. Find it!

- **Vendors**. Your vendors have a lot to teach you. Some of the people who sell you your products and services have been in the industry for many years and can offer you both advice and information. Even if they don't know much about your industry, they very likely know quite a bit about starting a company! Every businessperson I have ever met has offered me at least one tidbit of useful information. Become a sponge when talking to the people who support your operation.

- **New Hire Interviews**. You can learn an enormous amount from those that are experts in their fields. Quite often, the field is new to the entrepreneurs. This is a great way to learn.

- **Customers!** I purposefully left this for last because it is by far the most important source of information…and also the one most often ignored. Your customers are an endless source of vital knowledge and information. Every person who buys your product can tell you *why* (s)he bought, *who* (s)he considered buying from, his/her view of the *industry*, his/her *likes* and *dislikes*, the list goes on ad infinitum. If you are not interviewing your customers on a regular basis then you are absolutely ignorant of the dynamics of the market. No study can possibly give you the depth and color of the market like one pleased (or displeased) customer. Today, right now, pick of the phone and ask the customer why they buy. This one question can change your life!

The bottom line is this: If you ever hope to become successful in your industry, then you must become knowledgeable about *everything* that you do. Further, if you every want to raise money from a sophisticated investor then you are going to have to be able to answer virtually any question that comes your way. There are some very smart people in the business world, and they are going to ask you very hard questions. You don't want to be standing in front of these people with your mouth hanging open. You must 'learn to learn' and prove that you are up to the challenge of becoming #1!

Key takeaways:

- Spend at least ½ hour each day in dedicated learning.
- Identify all the skills and knowledge that are important to your field.
- Identify all the resources and people available.
- Answer the key questions in your industry. What is important to know?
- Humble yourself. You do NOT know everything, and never will.
- Become a 'learner' who is constantly seeking to add knowledge.
- Admit when you don't know something, then seek to learn about it.

Case 1: I don't know...

Scott is a driven guy. He knows what he wants and works 24/7 to get it. In the past Scott was also, however, a bit closed-minded. "I used to think I had it all sown up," Scott reflected. "I felt like there was nobody smarter than me. Boy was I wrong." To Scott's credit, there were reasons to believe he was 'the smartest guy in the room'. He was valedictorian of his undergraduate class at Harvard, and the top 10% of his Yale business school cohort. Scott's resume read like a power broker: Internship at the White House, investment banking for Goldman Sachs on Wall Street, and now CEO of a fast moving tech startup.

What Scott missed, however, was that there were many other smart people out there. "I really did not prepare that much for my investor pitches," Scott recalled. "I walked in feeling like I knew everything about my industry and that nobody had as much intelligence and understanding as I did. And then I met Karen." Karen Schlossberg was a partner at one of the top venture capital firms in Scott's industry, and was known for being able to pick a winner. According to Scott, "Karen literally ate me alive in my first pitch. She peppered me with questions so incisive that I felt like I was back in school trying to understand trigonometry. She pointed out flaws in my assumptions, quoted industry statistics I had never seen, and ripped apart my business model. At one point I actually stood there with my mouth hanging open. I was utterly humiliated."

Being a learning-oriented person, Scott took this as an opportunity to grow. "I never again will assume I know everything. Every day I try to read something new about my industry. Sure, most of it I already know, but every once and a while I read something that gives me an edge. Every day is an opportunity to pick up something new." Scott is currently the CEO of a very successful startup valued at over $300 million.

Case 2: Selling Like a Winner

This story involves my personal experience with learning. As I started my first company I was confronted with the proposition of selling a product that did not exist in a market that was undefined. I would walk into meetings with a mockup of my product, hoping that customers would buy based on what I promised they would get. It was tough going. I sold very little, and pushed myself financially to the breaking point. I simply did not have the skills to move a product that did not exist.

Luckily, a friend of mind had been taking sales training classes and was experiencing great success. He encouraged me to buy various sales tapes and books as a starting point. I went out and spent $100 (a large sum for me at that point) on Brian Tracy sales tapes. I listened to them on my way to every meeting. Then I got more tapes, started to read every morning, and enrolled in sales courses. The results were remarkable and very quick! Within 2 months I was selling something virtually every day, and by the end of the year I had sold 10 times what I expected to sell. I literally blew the cover off of my own expectations!

My new skills as a salesperson continue to pay off to this day. A few years ago I helped my partners raise over $50 million in financing in part by applying what I had learned from my sales training. I now teach small companies how to sell more effectively…even though I am not a salesperson by occupation. I simply decided to learn a skill that I thought might be useful, and the results literally changed my life! I now firmly believe that every entrepreneur, no matter what industry, should learn to sell as part of their own personal training. If you can't sell, you can't be successful.

LESSON 11: CASH FLOW IS KING

There are many things that seem contradictory in life, and this is one of them. First, there is the notion that you must have money to make money. Very true. In order to get loans, survive downturns and generally feel good about your security you should have at least some cash in the bank. If you have no money in the bank then you are at risk because you have no financial options. Investors will fleece you because they know they can. It is hard to be choosy when your 'runway' is very short. Ideally, you need to operate with at least 6 months of cash in the bank; that is, you can go for 6 months without *any* additional income.

This notion is directly contradicted, however, by another truth: You must spend money to make money. Another way to put this is: You can't cost-cut your way to growth. I have both experienced and seen an almost paranoid tendency among entrepreneurs that keeps them from spending *anything*, and this can be just as damaging as spending too much. While you do need to keep a good amount of cash in the bank, you also need to spend money on the things and people that will make you successful. This is the rub of growing a company….you must both stay safe and take risks.

As a bit of a digression, I should point out that this dichotomy exists in the very fabric of life itself. Every cell in nature has two basic impulses: One to keep the cell's boundaries stable and secure, and another to manage its interactions with the outside world in such a way as to stay connected. Both are accomplished through the cell wall. In this way each cell is both an individual entity and also an integral part of its community. Whenever the cell interacts with the surrounding world it risks overextending itself (like taking in toxins or poisons). It risks death. And yet if the cell puts up too much of a barrier and isolates itself from the outside world it will deprive itself of necessary nutrients. And so it risks death. Life is a balancing act between security and interaction.

I point all this out simply to show that your cash position is, like life, a balancing act. You need to both husband your cash (stay safe) *and* invest it in worthy projects (take risks). Your job is to manage this process so that you maximize safety and minimize risk…which is not always clear or easy. Some of the most stressful times I have experienced as an entrepreneur has occurred when the balance was uncertain, when I simply did not know the right answer. This stress is part of being a founder, and so I suggest you practice getting used to the feeling.

The key to managing this process is to become very aware of your cash flows…on a weekly basis if possible. Too many times I have been called in to help a struggling startup only to find that the founders have *absolutely no knowledge* of their own cash position. The entrepreneurs just keep working and spending hoping that at some point they will become 'successful' and not need to worry about cash. Then one day a large customer fails to pay their bill on time and the company risks bankruptcy. In a fit of panic the founders seek outside funding only to find that banks won't touch them and investors want to take half the company for a bridge loan.

Finding out the truth about your cash position can be both frightening and liberating. Sometimes founders are shocked at how little leeway (runway) they have. This knowledge is good and merely indicates a need to build a larger buffer. Other times founders are relieved because they see that they have better cash flows than they thought. This knowledge is also good and can indicate a need to be more conscious about investment and strategic growth. Either way, as a founder you should know on a moment-by-moment basis where you stand and how that affects your risk profile.

Ask yourself the following questions:

1. When can we *realistically* expect to start bringing in revenue?
2. How long could we go with *no* revenues?
3. What would happen if our largest customer did not pay on time?
4. If we needed to, how much cash could we accumulate?
5. Where do we spend most of our money?

6. What is our average cash position in any given month?
7. Do we pay our bills on time?
8. What is our cash position *right now*?
9. What are our options if we have a shortage of cash?

If you can't answer all of these questions, you don't have a good handle on your cash flow. When you don't know your cash flow, you can't make intelligent decisions about saving vs. spending. You are bound to fall out of balance because you have no idea where you are. It is like trying to stay upright on a listing ship…with your eyes closed. Open your eyes, get to know how your cash flows in and out, and then you can make good decisions.

To make this concept even more baffling, there are times when you actually need to spend even when you don't feel like you have adequate cash flow. This is the nature of a startup…spending money you don't have to increase the possibility of success. Creative and strategic risk taking. As an example, I am a consultant who helps startups become successful. Most of my clients have very little cash to spare when we first meet, and yet I encourage them to spend it with the faith that they will make much more than they spend. So they dip into savings, borrow, or get creative in order to secure my services. In the end they earn many multiples of what they ever spent on me because they learned how to become successful. This is a good use of limited cash.

I have also seen, however, entrepreneurs do very silly things like go into debt to pay for things that have no hope of bringing in revenue.

Borrowing in order to decorate your office is, frankly, stupid. Your nice new office will do *nothing* to make you successful. Your precious cash will be squandered on an ego trip. Every dime you have needs to be applied in a way that will move you forward, not keep you where you are.

In summation, your cash position is like your blood pressure. It must fall within a range in order for you to be healthy. Too high and you are not investing enough. Too low and you risk your enterprise. How and where you spend your money is an art form that must be mastered, and your daily cash position is information that you need to develop your skills.

Key Takeaways:

- Be able to operate for at least 6 months with minimal revenue, if possible.
- Know your cash position on a weekly basis.
- Don't hoard. Spend money on strategic growth.
- Cost-cutting will never grow your company.
- Be willing to take calculated risks with your cash. Occasionally you need to spend what you don't have in order to secure an opportunity.
- Always seek a balance between spending and saving. There is no magic formula. Develop your intuition.

Case 1: Belly up to the Trough!

Chris used to be a consultant for a large web development firm. He started with the company during the first few years of the 'dot com' boom, and rode the wave until the crash in 2000. "It was a crazy time," Chris recalled some years later. "There was so much money for web development it was incredible...we were swimming in cash! Our company wouldn't develop a web-site for less that $3 million, and people were paying it!" One of the more bizarre examples of this boom was an attempt to resurrect an old brand and turn it into a dotcom wonder.

In Chris's words: "The owners of this not-to-be named consumer brand decided to recreate the company as a web-based enterprise. We bid on the technical development project and won. The contract was over $11 million. We staffed the project with 50+ people. It was really a huge endeavor. Within a few weeks though, I saw that the whole company was a giant feed trough. The $150 million they had raised was going to company cars, plush offices and a HUGE executive corps. There were over 30 VP's in the company only 1 year in! We hadn't even finished the development before the company started running out of cash...and then the market bottomed out. The company ran out of money in just over a year. Today, there is nothing left. In my experience this is, hands down, the worst waste of cash ever."

Case 2: I thought you were my partner!

Sarah had been running her small company for 3 years, and had seen many ups and downs. "Cash flow was always an issue" she told us. "We had a publishing cycle that required a big outlay of cash before we could get paid. We were always biting our fingernails to make payroll during our spending period." Then one day Sarah saw a billboard ad from a local bank declaring that they were interested in working with small businesses. Excited, Sarah contacted the branch manager. Sarah recalled later that "The ads were very friendly! They said, essentially, 'We are your partner and want to help you grow'."

As hoped, Sarah was able to secure a $100 thousand credit line and stared using it immediately. "We were so relieved!" Sara recalled. "We could now manage our ups and downs without stress." A year or so later, however, the economy hit a snag and fell into recession. "I woke up one morning to a message from my bank," Sarah recounted. "They indicated they were closing credit lines that were deemed 'risky'. They asked me to pay off the entire balance within 2 weeks! We were right in the middle of our biggest cash outlay period and were at very serious risk of bankruptcy if we could not pay. It was the first time in my business life that I wept from stress." Sarah was eventually forced to borrow money from family members in order to pay back her credit line, and decided shortly after to sell her business.

"I will never again trust banks," Sarah vowed. "Or financiers generally. They are not out for your best interests. They are not your 'friends'. Now I always keep my credit lines low and only use them for very short-term needs. And although it seems crazy sometimes, I try to keep a chunk of cash in the bank just in case."

Case 3: Keeping the Runway

Keith had been to 'the show' many times. "I have been pitching investors on business ideas for over 10 years" Keith told us. "I know the game, and I know how important it is to pitch from a place of power." To give himself an edge Keith always keeps at least 6 months of operating cash in the bank. "I never go into a pitch meeting immediately needing money," Keith emphasized. "The investors can smell your fear a mile away. If my idea is not yet funded I make it clear that I personally have enough in the bank to make it for at least a year without investors. If I already have a company and it is not yet making money, I won't pitch unless I know I can keep going for 6 months without any additional revenue.".

Having a 6 month 'runway' for himself and the company allows Keith to pitch with confidence. "And I know," Keith laughs, "what a shark investor will do once they sense a company running out of money! They will drag the process along for months until the company becomes truly desperate. Then they will start forcing them to drop the price. It is an old game that I refuse to play." As of today Keith has started and funded 5 successful companies and continues to enjoy a great relationship with the investment community. "I like a lot of these guys, but I also know that they would steal my first-born if they could. It's just part of the business."

Case 4: Leap of Faith

5 years ago a client came to me in a very stressed state. She and her husband were having severe financial difficulties and were not sure if they were going to be able to pay their mortgage. Even so, she had a dream of owning a company and believed that she had both the skills and persistence to make it happen. She just needed some guidance to get off the ground because she could not afford to make any mistakes. The business needed to start making money immediately in order for her and her family to live.

Given her financial condition I was skeptical that she would be willing to pay my fees. My services, even though I know they are effective, are not inexpensive. She was going to have to take a fairly sizable risk with her precious cash, and I knew from experience this was going to be stressful.

As part of my process I ask each client if they are prepared to commit to themselves completely, to let go of all reservations, and to be willing to create a successful life. And although you might think this is a 'no-brainer' answer, I have found many people are not ready to do this. My client's answer was a firm 'yes', and she began to make her payments and participate in her own growth. Today her business is worth $10 million.

I have learned through my work with many, many start-ups that cash, when committed with intention and purpose, can literally change lives. Saving cash can be helpful, but it can also limit your ability to succeed. I now encourage all of my clients to see every check they send me as an investment in themselves...not the payment of a bill. If you can see your expenditures this way you will be able to choose more wisely and know that you are increasing the likelihood of success.

Case 5: Picking the Right Project

Nina was in a quandary. Her startup was very close to finishing what she thought would be a market-leading product, but the company was also running out of money and the investors were getting skittish. More, a potential major customer had approached Nina and asked for her product...except with major custom work. "This job would have brought in much needed cash, but it also would have taken my team off-track for at least 6 months," Nina related. "It seemed like a Faustian bargain, buying short term cash for a longer-term product launch disruption."

In the end Nina chose to do the custom work and take the cash. "It turned out to be a big mistake," Nina said later. "We got about 6 months of additional runway, but the project allowed a competitor to beat us to market. Now our competitor has a valuation of over $100 millio, while we are struggling to produce a new and better version to beat their offering. If I had it to do over, I would seek more cash from our investors or some other source...anything to get the product out. We could have beaten our competitor if we had not been so desperate."

LESSON 12: AN EXIT STRATEGY IS A FAILURE STRATEGY

The term 'exit strategy' is a cringe-inducing phrase for me. In short, it means 'how am I going to exit my company and make a lot of money'. In my opinion this is the best way to *decrease* your odds of creating something worthy of being bought. If you are starting a company in order to 'exit' it, then you are basically telling yourself and your investors that you could care less about what you create…you just want the money. And when you are doing things just for the money you are more likely to cut corners, give up when things get tough, and otherwise do things that don't make sense in the long term. You cannot plan your exit, you can only build a product that customers want and do so while making a profit.

Trying to plan your exit is so ridiculous that I teach my entrepreneurs to not even entertain the thought. The real truth is that *any* plan, even one extremely well researched and assembled, is wrong the moment you finish it. Yes, you heard me: Your plan is wrong. Here are some stats for you: 41% of Harvard Business School (HBS) entrepreneurs said that their start-ups ended up taking twice as long and twice as much capital as they had planned, and 79% said execution took longer than planned. Only 4% of all business plans were on target. And I am willing to bet that even those 4% had aspects of their plans that were incorrect.

So how can you possibly plan for an event that is contingent upon what other companies might do in response to your success? You have no idea if/when/how another company might want to buy you in two to five years. You can't possibly know even six months from now if the product you are selling today will be of interest to your customers. Can you see every innovation in your market for the next five years? Every competitor's actions? Or guess the state of the economy? It is absurd to believe you can 'plan an exit'.

Even if you had all the information in the world, I still recommend you not even speak about an exit plan. To speak of exiting your company is like planning the death of your child…to do so shakes the very foundation of what you are trying to create. Once you start a company you have given birth to a living thing. Your start-up is a legal entity standing on its own. If you want someone to give you a lot of money for it you need to pour love into it, nurture it, and have great dreams for it. Certainly you can plan for its success, but you can't control the situations it will experience. Life is life, and anything can happen. Your job is to support, love and invest in your creation to the best of your ability and then let go of any attachment to the outcome.

Psychologically, when people attach to outcomes they live in an almost constant state of stress. When you do something in the world and then *expect* the world to respond the way you want it to respond then you are inevitably disappointed. This disappointment, if experienced often enough, can become frustration, fear or rage. Over time these negative energies wear you down and sap your strength. The only answer is to do your best and *let go*. Your company may be worth a billion dollars in 5 years…or worth nothing. You have no idea. You can only plan to the best of your ability and doing what you can do *today* to make your 'baby' successful.

If this were not enough, when you dream about exiting your company you tend to create that reality. Your subconscious mind, which is 95% of your mental processing, responds to the subtle message of 'exit' and begins to act accordingly. If you have ever played golf, for instance, you know that the worst thing you can do during your shot is to think about 'not hitting that house'. Inevitably your shot will veer in the direction of what you are thinking. This is true of everything in your life: You create what you think about. When you think about an 'exit', then, you tend to create exactly that…but because you cannot predict with any certainty you will have no idea what type of exit you will get. Your subconscious mind will simply try to end the thing you say you are trying to create, in any way it can. This can become a form of unconscious self-sabotage.

As you think about your business, then, you must focus on one thing: Creating an amazing human system that produces high-quality products that meet your customers' needs. If you end up getting bought, going public, merging with another company…whatever…it will be because you built something valuable, not because you planned the exit. You must strongly envision that which you want to create, clearly intend your course, and then take action to create it. All physical manifestation works this way, and your company will be no different.

I recommend that all my clients create a 'vision story' about the future of their business. This story is a dialogue about what you intend to create in the future, but told in the present tense. For example I might write this: "I am walking into my offices Monday morning and enjoying the light streaming in from the huge windows. There are plants all around, and the atmosphere is welcoming. The air is crackling with creative anticipation as our 80 employees work with joy and excitement. Our revenues are surpassing $xx this quarter and will grow even more in the future. Our customers love our products and working with us. My executive team…etc." The key is to tell the story with as much color and detail as you can. Use excited, emotional language to get your body behind it. Inspire yourself! When you do this you are telling your subconscious mind to begin working on what you have written. Behind the scenes your body will begin to accept your vision as reality and act accordingly. Literally, your mind will find a way to create what you have thought.

Visioning has been proven effective in virtually every human endeavor. But you must make sure your visioning is *positive*, and not the reverse. Every thought you have, every plan you make, every act you take needs to move you toward that which you have pictured in your mind. If you attempt to control the outcomes, however, you will be inevitably disappointed. You cannot force a company to acquire you or control your customers' purchasing habits. You can only do your best, work hard, and then let go. Over time you will see that your 'exit' either becomes unnecessary or a pleasant surprise.

Key takeaways:

- 'Exit strategies' do not create viable businesses.
- Focus on creating a great company with a great culture that produces great products.
- The value you create will attract investors and buyers.
- Plan your business and execute, but let go of control. You cannot force your success.
- Your plan is likely wrong the moment it is finished. Constantly learn and adapt.
- Clearly envision that which you are trying to create. Write a 'vision story' with color and excitement. Your emotion and excitement is a powerful creator.
- Let your 'exit' make itself known over time. It will eventually become obvious.

Case 1: Show me the money!

Joe is an incredibly energetic guy. He is always moving fast and focusing on what he can do to make money. When he started his first company he was very focused on building something he could sell to someone so that he could make a lot and retire...whatever that meant. His brothers used to say that he was born looking for cash, and did not really have the patience to wait for it. A natural salesperson, Joe thrived in business until he decided he wanted to go off on his own.

At first Joe did really well. He pre-sold his products and built a large customer base. His revenues were going through the roof and within a year he had 20 people working for him. Then his impatience took over. Joe started cutting corners in order to increase his margins and 'nickel and dimed' his customers at every turn. One of his former employees said later that, "Joe simply could not wait. He wanted to be super wealthy today and could not stand the idea that he had to build a well-functioning company first. He thought the overnight 'internet billionaire' model applied to all industries."

In the second year Joe's corner cutting started to take its toll. The company developed a reputation in the industry for being 'shady' and customers began to push back about quality. Then the Feds stepped in. It turns out Joe had begun to make 'side bets' with company money that were not entirely legal. Joe's investors filed a suit, and by the end of the year the company was in liquidation. "I guess Joe got what he wanted," the former employee recounts. "He has his early retirement!"

Case 2: Good to Great

Prakash had just been burned by a former business partner and decided to try to build something on his own. "I was really disillusioned," Prakash said later. "I had been working with my partner for 2 years and then he sold the company out from under me. His deal minimized the value of the ownership shares and maximized his pay as the head of a major group at the acquiring company. Essentially, I got nothing and he is getting a giant salary." In response Prakash was determined to build a company that stood for something bigger that money.

"As I wrote down my intentions, I made sure to focus on service over anything else," Prakash recalled. "I wanted my company to be 'of service' to my customers, my employees and my investors. My company would be more than good…it would be Great in the way that lasting enterprises are: Honest, caring, growth-oriented, service-oriented and dedicated to providing value to customers. Essentially, I wanted the 'triple bottom line' of profit, social good, and employee happiness." Many of Prakash's friends and family thought he was crazy to be so socially minded, but he was undeterred.

"I am focused on changing the business landscape and I have a long term view," Prakash says today. "I want to build something based on love, not self-benefit. Sure, I intend to make money, but I will not do it at anyone's expense." Today Prakash is 5 years into his business and is due to hit $10 million in revenues next year. He has been contacted by buyers in his industry but is still determined to create something powerful on his own. "I see this as a world-wide mission," he says. "I intend to build something that will be seen as a positive example for generations."

LESSON 13: COMMUNICATION SKILLS ARE ABSOLUTELY CRITICAL

In my experience, one of the greatest impediments to group performance is the inability to communicate. By this I don't mean the *literal* inability to communicate - obviously people are able to talk and email and share – but instead the inefficiency created when people do not adequately understand each other and spend inordinate time in either conflict or repeated attempts to clarify a position. This type of *mis*communication is like a tax on the organization, it slows down performance and drains energy from the team members.

The reason this is such a problem is because most people don't even know it is happening. We think we are having good conversations and that we are understood, and then get angry or frustrated when our message does not seem to sink in. Conflicts erupt because people are either a) sending information in a way that does not work or b) blocking the receipt of that information through poor listening habits. Either way, information that should flow easily from person to person is 'gummed up' by the inability to communicate in a way that encourages genuine connection.

Here are just a few examples of how poor communication manifests in the workplace:

In person:

- Manager or leader imparts directional instructions (i.e. we need to do xyz), and those instructions are misinterpreted. Work is not completed as desired.
- Employee is left out of a meeting. Hurt feelings and resentment result in decreased productivity.
- Valued team member feels unappreciated and yet is unable to express what (s)he feels, or is not heard in his/her issue. Team member quits for a 'better' situation.
- 'Water cooler' talk is the only way to learn about what is happening at the company, so a culture of hidden conversations, gossip, and mistrust develops.
- Leaders withhold information about the company in order to maintain a sense of control over what people experience. The information leaks anyway and trust in leadership is broken.

Phone:

- A customer calls to complain about a poor experience and

employees, fearful of difficult conversations, let the calls go to voicemail.

- Managers leave negative feedback on someone's voicemail and then do not respond to employee's calls.
- Salespeople are afraid to make 'cold-calls' for fear of upsetting the prospect. Days go by with no outgoing voice communication from sales department.

Email/text

- Disputes are aired through group emails. Conflict occurs indirectly with each participant on the chain sniping at all the others. Hours are wasted crafting accusations and responses.
- Long emails go unread because none of the recipients has the time to find the parts that are relevant to them. Time is wasted crafting the email because they go unread, while even more time is wasted because the point or directive within the email is not received.
- Short texts or emails are sent about an inflammatory subject. The recipient is left to 'read into' the tone of the message and so walks away confused or insulted. Hurt feelings result in lost focus and work stoppages.

In the end human communication is inherently imperfect because we are all individuals trying to convey what we are thinking and feeling, and words sometimes cannot convey that very well. Yet we can all develop the skill to communicate and listen in a way that maximizes the likelihood of an efficient exchange and thereby increases the productivity of the group. If every person on the planet was able to communicate perfectly, for example, then we would all be understood. If we were all understood then there would be a much lower tendency toward conflict because we would 'get' where the other person is coming from.

Your job as the leader of an organization, no matter how small, is to continue to develop your communication skills and culture in order to allow information to flow freely and openly between all members of the group. I like to call this 'perfect transparency', where everyone is completely open with everyone else about everything. Another term is 'intimacy', which is when people feel comfortable enough with each other to share their deepest selves. Certainly, this is a lofty goal in a business organization. Open sharing is not all that common. Yet if you want to maximize efficiency you must learn how to both give and receive information in an open, honest and transparent way.

I have some rules of thumb that I use to guide my clients' thinking in this respect:

1. Never hide information from your team.
2. Learn how to have difficult conversations effectively, and always face to face.
3. A leader's listening/speaking ratio must be 75/25
4. Speak with inspiration and excitement.
5. Emails should be no longer than 4 sentences.
6. If nobody has any issues, then you are likely not listening well

enough.
7. Bad news is always best delivered in person or at least over the phone.

A trusting relationship or culture can only be built when communication between all parties is completely respectful and transparent. You may think this is easy, but in reality it takes patience and constant practice. There are literally hundreds of excellent books on the subject (my recommendation is "Crucial Conversations" by Kerry Patterson, et. al.) but I can give you a starting point here.

Generally there are two aspects of communication: Intake and outflow. Listening/reading is the intake portion and is by far the most important...especially listening. Speaking/writing is the outflow component and is important to learn how to do in an effective way because without these skills your message is lost. Non-verbal communication (facial expressions, body language, etc.) is also very important and can sometimes contain just as much information as the verbal type, but for now I will just focus on the latter.

Good listening should be a centerpiece of your skills as a leader. If you can't listen well, then you can't gather information necessary to make good decisions. There is great truth to the saying 'the smartest person in the room is the one not speaking'. When you speak your brain literally shuts off your ability to hear, and so you miss the goldmine of information around you in every moment. Salespeople need to learn how to listen to customers in order to understand their needs. Leaders need to listen to their executive team in order to understand the state of the organization. Managers need to listen to their teams in order to know the status of projects and team morale. In my experience, the *inability to listen is one of the greatest leadership failings commonly practiced by business people.*

Good listening requires an ability to focus on another person *completely*. An excellent listener is patient and able to put away their own desire to speak in order that another can be fully heard. Strong listeners also are able to *reflect* what they hear in order to confirm to the speaker that the message was received. In my experience this type of listening is incredibly powerful. It can sell products, eliminate complaining, and bring invaluable intelligence into the organization. *If you are not listening you are not learning, and if you are not learning you are not growing.*

The second, slightly less important aspect of communication is speaking/writing. To speak and write well is very effective, but only after the listeners have been heard and believe that you understand them. If you speak before you understand, people will generally shut you out. So the mantra is 'listen first, speak after understanding'.

I evaluate verbal and written communication in three ways: Clarity, safety and inspiration. Clarity is the ability to transfer information simply and concisely, using as few words as possible and to greatest effect. Long, blathering speeches and emails are ineffective. You must learn to be clear and purposeful in your communication. The second one, safety, is the ability to create a respectful environment for your words. In order to create safety for the listener you must be able to let them know that you care about them and want them to be successful…before you speak. And when you do speak, it must be in a way that conveys information without insult. You can be stern, but you need not be insulting. Safety creates a space where the listener can hear *anything*.

The last area, inspiration, is the hardest for many people and yet can also be the most effective. Inspiration means to literally 'breathe Spirit into' something. When you speak in an inspiring way you appeal to the highest good in others, to their dreams and aspirations. Inspirational speaking requires that you find the excitement, joy and hope within yourself (and sometimes anger) such that you can emotionally *move* others. When done well an inspirational speaker can move thousands of people in a positive (or negative) direction. This type of speaking can raise millions of dollars, sell thousands of products and inspire hundreds of workers. Learn to do this well and you can move people to do anything!

This is a VERY short primer on communication, but the point remains the same. If you want to create an effective, powerful organization, then you must learn to communicate well. If you want your team to be effective, then you must constantly train them in the art of information transfer. Communication skills are not something you learn once and then forget…they are something that will continually affect your life and business. They must be practiced constantly. I encourage you to start this process today and spend time on it periodically for the rest of your life. Your business depends on it!

Key Takeaways:

- The inability to communicate well is the source of most organizational friction and inefficiency.
- Most people think they communicate well, but in reality they don't have the skills.
- As a leader you must learn to take in and send out information in a way that maximizes understanding.
- Ongoing communication training is necessary to create an effective culture.
- Develop rules for communication to minimize friction
- Listen more than you speak. Use 75/25 ratio.
- Practice communicating clearly, safely and with inspiration.
- Your businesses productivity will be determined by you and your employees ability to communicate effectively!

Case 1: Telling is not selling

James is a funny, gregarious and highly likable guy. He is also salesperson who is very knowledgeable about his products. The problem is that James does not know when to shut up. In sales meetings James can joke and laugh with customers, but he has a very hard time listening to what the customer is trying to say. "James is a force of nature," his manager recalled, "and like a hurricane, he can be overwhelming. I sat in on meetings with James and watched as he talked and talked about our products and how great we were. Sure, the customers loved him and laughed at his jokes, but he would walk out having no knowledge of the customer's needs."

Over time James's sales numbers proved lackluster, and so his manager decided to enroll him in communication training. The training worked for a short time, but James's habits were just too strong. According to his manager, "I think I made a mistake in enrolling him, and only him, in only one course. In retrospect we should have had larger organizational involvement. James needed the support of the whole team to change his habits, and our culture was just not that listening-oriented. If I were going to do it over I would have asked for team wide training over a long period." In the end James was let go. "I really felt bad about that," his manager recalled. "He was a good guy with a lot of potential. We should have taken this a bit more seriously than we did."

Case 2: The Email Roundabout

"We had an ongoing nightmare on our hands," Nina recalled with a grimace. *"Behind the scenes of our fast moving company was a never ending battle. Every complaint was being aired publicly and lived for days longer than it should have."* Being the HR manager of a 50-person startup, Nina was in charge of corporate culture and was tasked with keeping up morale during stressful times. The problem was she could not seem to keep control of the rampant e-mail 'rants' that people were using to let off steam.

"Our workforce was fairly distributed," Nina related to us later, *"and so communication could be sporadic and difficult. Over time 'camps' began to form as sales felt pitted against our tech developers, and operations got frustrated with marketing. Our CEO was not a strong internal communicator, and so everyone started questioning and commenting through e-mail. I would find out days after the event that 10 people in the company had been having a running e-mail battle about some silly topic that could have been resolved in one phone call. I got ahold of one of these email strings at some point and it was pages and pages long! There must have been 30-40 hours of work in some of these diatribes!"*

After speaking with the leadership team about the problem, Nina decided to institute a dramatic solution. A note went out from the CEO saying that there would be a new rule: All disputes, of either process or interaction, were to be conducted by phone or in person. Any person violating this rule would be given 1 warning and then let go. *"Overnight the problem stopped,"* Nina remembers. *"Overall morale began to improve. Since people had to actually talk to each other their communications became more respectful and cooperative. We even started to have conversations about communication norms and style. It was one of the best decisions we ever made!"*

Case 3: Walking the talk

Sean is the founder and CEO of an eco-friendly products startup. He prides himself in the consciousness of his company when it comes to all aspects of business, including his internal communications. "One of our core values is being open and transparent," Sean relates. "Nothing is off the table communication-wise." One day, however, Sean's principles were tested. "One of our employee's commented during a weekly company 'town hall' that everyone's salaries and stock ownership percentages were hidden. This person pointed out a contradiction between our values and actions...we said we were open yet did not disclose how much everyone was making. It was true."

In response, Sean declared that they would have a special series of meetings to talk about transparency and openness regarding salary and ownership. They established a 'transparency committee' to accumulate the results and then report back on what they heard at a future company meeting. "The results were very interesting," Sean remembers. "Not everyone wanted to have that information shared. In the end the results were about 60% in favor of sharing the information, with 40% against." When the rest of the company saw the results there was a heated conversation about the fairness of forcing others to share information against their will, and it became clear to Sean that keeping the salary and ownership information personal was the best idea considering all viewpoints.

Sean, however, recalls a more important outcome of the process: "Going through that exercise may have seemed like a time waste to other CEO's, but I found it exceptionally productive. It turns out that the process was more important than the outcome. By having an open conversation about a difficult topic we built trust. Even if the outcome was not what everyone wanted, people felt involved and heard. Our culture took a huge step forward that day. Months later I still have employees telling me how much those meetings meant to them." Sean's company continues to grow and thrive today, and his employees regularly say that they feel like it is the best place they have ever worked.

LESSON 14: LAWYERS ARE FOR EMERGENCIES ONLY

I have nothing against lawyers, and in fact count many as among my closest friends. They provide a very valuable service in helping businesspeople create agreements, think through potential risks, and build lasting business structures. Lawyers are an inherent part of any society built upon the rule of law: They are the technicians of a system built to ensure fairness among our society's members. They also, however, can be a tax on a system if the people using them cannot resolve disputes in a way that is constructive and connected. There is a saying in martial arts that 'if you find yourself in a fight you have already lost'. This is also true of the legal system. If you find yourself in court over a business dispute, then you have already lost. The lawyers are going to cost you much more than anything you would have forfeited in a negotiated settlement.

One of the main reasons people use lawyers to resolve conflicts is because they are afraid of the connection required to resolve a difficult issue. Instead of working with someone constructively and directly, they use proxies to relay their positions. Rather than compromise, they try to force their positions using a more powerful intermediary. You can see these power-plays at the individual level all the way up to the scale of societies and countries. An embittered husband hiring a crackerjack lawyer is no different than a country using its army to eliminate an enemy. Both cases are a failure of what psychologists call 'intimacy', or the ability to relate to another human being in a way that creates understanding and connection.

'Intimacy' is a tough word. Most people, not surprisingly, think of it in sexual terms. This is a misunderstanding. I believe it is a word that we must increasingly use in our vernacular because it conveys something that many of us find uncomfortable: That in order to live together in a peaceful way we must get to know and respect each other at an 'intimate' level. We must seek to understand, to empathize and to connect. If we cannot do these things then we are left to stand behind our individual walls and throw rocks at one another. We sit isolated in a sea of humanity, using physical and social barriers to make sure the 'other' does not get the best of us.

Look around our world. Notice the gated communities established to keep out the 'undesirables'. Count the number of weapons we buy in order to protect ourselves against 'them'. Listen to the news stories about attacks, epidemics and wars that 'those others' are causing. Observe the reactions of people when they drive through 'that part of town'. We are surrounded by fear of each other. This fear gives us reason to increase our vigilance, to keep everyone at bay except those who we deem safe. And even then, the safest of our people can turn out to be our enemies. Our wives or husbands turn into persecutors, our neighbors pedophiles, our families disloyal, our pastors or business leaders untrustworthy. How often do we live in fear of each other, and what are the consequences?

Ultimately, we each pay the price for our separation. The fear of each other creates an anger that excludes understanding. We say 'I won't even *talk* to that jerk', and seclude ourselves in our own thoughts and opinions. Anyone who does not agree with us is an enemy unworthy of our attention and care. And because we are all inherently different we eventually find that *everyone* is an enemy. We stay utterly alone in our 'cohort of 1'. We sit in our fortress of righteousness lamenting the stupidity and wrongness of everyone that does not share our views. It is a lonely and empty existence.

If you want proof of our separation, simply look at the prevalence of three things: Weapons, drugs and lawsuits. Weapons presume an evil and angry world bent on our destruction. When we have a weapon we can 'repel' all those who we deem dangerous. Drugs, on the other hand, keep us from experiencing reality and allow us to soothe the emptiness we feel from our own separation. The prevalence of anti-anxiety, anti-depression and painkilling medications is testament to our aloneness. And in any plaintiff's lawsuit you can almost hear, if you listen carefully, the demand of someone seeking to be heard in his/her pain. 'I feel wronged and want to be acknowledged' could be the opening statement in every civil suit.

In the business world this separation manifests as a temptation to use lawyers to settle disputes, a process that is akin to using money to buy love. In the end a lot of mistrust is created doing something that could have been done quite easily, naturally and for free if only ego had been surrendered. Resolving disputes is only difficult because you see yourself as right and the other wrong. If you can drop this and genuinely try to understand others then lawyers and lawsuits become necessary only when you are truly being threatened…only when you have already 'lost'.

I have been involved in legal disputes, and I have learned the hard way how much one simple misunderstanding can cost. It is so easy in the beginning of a conflict to write another person off, to simply say 'they are jerks' and contact a lawyer. After all, 'I am right' and 'they are wrong', so let's prove it in court. The problem is that contacting a lawyer is easy…it is the rest of the process that is hard. Most people have never been through the process and so don't understand that legal disputes take *years*, not months. Even the simplest case involves evidence gathering, discovery, depositions, preliminary hearings, arbitration, full hearings, appeals and so on. At each stage you will dedicate hundreds of hours to the process and pay your attorneys an endless stream of fees. If you have not gone bankrupt you will likely have neglected your business to the point where it will fail anyway.

The personal toll is just as great. The stress, I can tell you from experience, is almost overwhelming. Years of strategizing, maneuvering, arguing and settling can eat at your health as well as your pocketbook. The price of separation is very high, and you will pay it if you choose this path. Once a legal dispute finally completes, virtually nobody is smiling except the lawyers. Even the winners walk away exhausted and demoralized.

I paint this picture for you in order that you hesitate for a moment before you call your lawyer to settle a dispute. As a small business owner you cannot afford to spend your precious time and money on a process that is a lose-lose for everyone. Instead you must be smart and resolve your disputes in a way that truly solves the problem, even if it means putting your ego to the side.

Intimacy, the act of connecting to another human being, requires that you step outside of yourself and seek to understand the perspective of another person. When you understand someone deeply, their hostility tends to diminish because they feel heard. They are less likely to attack because you have connected with them in their loneliness and pain. It is much more difficult to be continually violent or aggressive with someone whom we count as a friend, so if you would like to avoid lawsuits and ongoing conflicts the only answer is to seek to understand and connect. Only then can you resolve.

Many of my clients misinterpret intimacy as 'giving in'. They think that if they give the person space to speak or to vent their anger then they have somehow lost. The idea of winning or losing in human relations is an ego-based concept. There is no winner or loser, just two or more people sharing. Nor does intimacy mean you are supposed to doing everything another person wants you to do! You are merely listening with an open mind and heart…you are not 'giving up' anything! Part of intimacy is sharing what YOU want as well, which deserves equal consideration. The point of creating intimacy is to lower the barriers to understanding and to allow the free flow of information. Based on the information you receive you may still decide to move forward with a formal dispute. Just give the dialogue a chance and see if you can diffuse the situation before it costs you your company.

There are many books on intimacy, conflict resolution and healthy dialogue, but each of them largely boils the process down to this:

1. **Connect**. Speak with the person face to face, or on the phone at a minimum. Minimize distance as much as possible, and be willing to let down your defenses.
2. **Listen**. Always seek to hear another person deeply. Don't listen to *respond*; instead, listen to *understand.*
3. **Mirror**. Repeat back what you have heard so that the speaker knows they are understood. Acknowledge the other's position (this does not mean *agreeing* with the position, but simply *acknowledgment* that it exists).
4. **Create Safety**. Clarify that your intention is to come to resolution, and that you want the other person to be happy

with it. You want a win-win. In order to do this you must let go of your ego's desire to win at the expense of the other. This lowers the other person's defenses and allows for a conversation.

5. **Speak personally.** When you do speak, talk from your own experience and needs, not from accusation. It is tempting to speak from a '*you* did...' or '*you* are...' perspective. Stick with the 'I feel...' or 'I need...' point of view. Use a tone of voice that is patient and kind, but also firm and resolved.

6. **Maximize benefit.** Once you understand the other person's perspective you can try to make sure both parties benefit. Let go of your ego and seek to create a lasting solution.

7. **Express gratitude.** As much as you might dislike the person you are dealing with, be grateful that they are willing to avoid open warfare. Who knows, you may just find a friend in the process...or at the very least you will change someone from hating you to being indifferent to you.

One thing that helps in this process is to remember that beneath *anger* lies *hurt*, and beneath *hurt* lies *fear*. If you can understand that an angry person is really just a scared person you can see their expression less as an attack and more as a call for understanding. Angry people mainly want to be understood in their pain, but don't know a more productive way to express that pain. Once you see the truth of a person's hurt you can work with them in a way that solves rather than inflames the problem.

When working with tough-minded, competitive business people, I find the biggest impediment to this process is the Ego. After all, it is not easy to speak kindly with a hostile person, especially if that person seems bent on attacking your most important creations. Yet it is also the only way to diffuse what can turn out to be an ongoing and expensive war. Throughout history man has gotten into conflicts that, upon later reflection, turned out to be colossal wastes of time and money. Don't repeat history! Develop the skill of being intimate with the people around you and use lawyers only when there is absolutely no other option!

Key Takeaways:

- Ongoing conflict is expensive and destructive.
- Anger is really just fear and pain made socially acceptable.
- The legal system is a *system* that once engaged can take years and hundreds of thousands of dollars.
- The use of lawyers as a first resort shows an inability or unwillingness to engage with those with whom we disagree.
- Resolving conflict with people requires *intimacy*. Intimacy is the act of connecting with someone in order to deeply understand the other's perspective, and to share yours.
- Your ego will fight intimacy because it wants to be *right*. It wants to *win*.
- War in any form is a failure of humanity's ability to be intimate with each other.
- Being intimate does not mean giving in, it merely means

deeply understanding another's position. Your position matters just as much if not more.

- Learning to communicate while in disagreement is a skill that can save you a huge amount of time and money. It is a meta-leadership skill that can determine your success!

Case 1 Part A: The Misunderstanding

Martin wondered how things could have gone so wrong so fast. He had just started his own company in clean tech and now he was facing a $50 million lawsuit.

A mechanical engineer by training, Martin had invented a new type of wind turbine that was significantly smaller and cheaper than other models in the market. He formed the company and started looking for co-founders who could take care of marketing and sales. A week or so later Martin met Kelly, a marketing exec for a big multinational company. Kelly was instantly interested in Martin's venture. Martin didn't know Kelly at all, but thought he credentials were impressive, and he liked Kelly's enthusiasm.

Knowing that choosing a co-founder was a big step, Martin arranged to meet with Kelly for a half day for coffee and brainstorming. "He got the concept right away", Martin related, "and he had some really good ideas on how to improve the turbine." While Martin liked many of Kelly's ideas, he thought they would only make sense in a later generation of the product. According to Martin, "I really didn't want to shut him down because he was so excited, so I acknowledged his ideas and suggested he come on board as a co-founder." Kelly seemed amenable and said he would think it over.

A few days later, Kelly called and decided he was going to stay with his current company, but wanted to keep in touch as Martin moved forward. Martin agreed and re-connected after 6 months to ask Kelly to be an investor. "He seemed really interested in the project, and I was excited about potentially having him on board," Martin said later.

Martin relates what happened next: "Kelly sent me an email saying that it was unfair that I was asking him to invest because he had significantly contributed to the design of the product. He wanted a portion of the company for what he believed was his contribution."

Martin was shocked. He had come up with the idea long before meeting Kelly, and nothing Kelly had said or offered was included in the design. In fact, Martin had come to the conclusion that Kelly's suggestions did not even fit into future designs, and so would be discarded. Martin responded to Kelly via email and stated his position that he, Martin, was sole owner of the idea and that he was shocked that Kelly would think otherwise.

Three weeks went by with no response from Kelly, until Martin heard a knock. "I open the door and was served a summons," Martin related. "I almost got sick. I wondered what in the world I had done so wrong as to be involved in a lawsuit. I rarely even argue with people!"

Case 1 Part B: A Second Chance

After recovering from his shock, Martin found a litigator who could help with the suit and the following day met with her legal team. "They were an impressive group, and asked all the right questions," Martin said. "But they came back to me with a shocking suggestion: Talk to Kelly. They said that before I paid the tens – or hundreds – of thousands in legal fees, that I really should reach out once more." Luckily Kelly and his attorney agreed, and Martin resolved to make the most of this opportunity.

In the meeting, Martin realized after listening to Kelly that he had never fully shared the details of what was in the product. Martin told me, "Kelly was proceeding under the false assumption that we were using his ideas. We weren't, but he didn't know that." Once they understood each other, Martin and Kelly came to an agreement where Kelly would be notified if Martin moved forward with any of his ideas, and be able to either a) deny their use or b) be given royalties on any resulting sales.

A few days later Kelly's attorney called to say they had signed the agreement and dropped the suit. "I have rarely ever felt so relieved," Martin said later. "I was fully prepared to enter into a battle that would have very likely cost me everything. I learned a huge lesson not only about handling risk, but more importantly about how to work with people before a simple misunderstanding gets out of hand."

Case 2: Early Diffusion

Standing in her company's trade show booth, Lauren was shocked at her competitor's aggressiveness. "He essentially threatened me with a lawsuit over a perceived patent infringement," she recounted. "It was about as sinister as you can get. He stood there with his lawyer, speaking in very threatening tones. Clearly he was trying to intimidate me." Rather than get upset and return his threats, Lauren decided to turn on the charm. "I smiled and asked him to explain his side of things. I listened very carefully and repeated what I heard, without admitting he was right. I just tried to be as accessible and open as possible."

After about ten minutes of listening, her competitor visibly softened. "It was like all the fight drained out of him. I started to see how he was just trying to protect his business from our superior products. I assured him that I thought we could both be successful in the market and that I wanted the best for him. In the end he actually gave me a hug and complimented my company!" Lauren now trains her staff and salespeople in the art of diffusing conflict. "It is truly remarkable what a little TLC will do to an angry or hurt person. Not many people really like being hostile. Deep down most of us want to be friends!"

LESSON 15: GET COMFORTABLE WITH RISK

One of the most common conversations I have with new entrepreneurs concerns their perception of risk and the decisions that it drives them to make. For example, many people who would like to start a company are reluctant to leave their existing jobs. They argue that it is 'safer' to work for a salary while building a business plan and getting initial funding. Only then, their reasoning goes, will they leave their job and go full time on their new venture. The logic may *seem* sound, but in reality they are merely shifting risk from one area to another. They are assuming that a known risk (not leaving their job) is better than an unknown risk (starting a company), and that seems to make them feel more comfortable.

Yet in life, everything is a risk. The moment you were conceived you were at risk of some catastrophic development in your mother's womb. As you entered the world you immediately stepped into an unknown space where 'things happen'. Throughout your life you have grown and lived and, if you are reading this book, successfully avoided the things that might have killed you. The fact is that you live with risk *all the time*. You cannot avoid it, and you cannot control it. You can hide in your house for the remainder of your life and *still* be at risk of any number of events…you just don't know.

Coming to terms with risk is important because if you over-plan for it you can actually increase your risk in other ways. Using the start-up example, when you decide to keep your job while starting a company you actually increase your risk of failure. How? Because when you keep your job you are sending a message to your customers, your future investors and yourself that you are *not fully committed*. When you give yourself the option to stay where you are, you say to the world 'not yet' and the world responds accordingly. You will flounder until you go all in. Your attempt to minimize the risks actually *increases* them.

Like life itself, the startup process is inherently risky. You are creating something new, something that will have ripple effects into the future. Your life will change in ways that you cannot possibly predict. Accept this. *Embrace* it. See every risk as an opportunity and *dive in*.

Now, I know that there are some risks that are less dangerous than others. There are things that any intelligent person would not do. These are the 'known' risks. You know, for example, that if you are trying to start a company you should probably not spend all your savings on a stuffed animal collection. This would be silly because the consequences are known and controllable.

On the other hand, you may decide to spend your money on a marketing campaign that might, or might not, be a waste of money. You don't know the outcome because you have never tried. In this case you must become comfortable with the risk and seek to learn from whatever you experience. You take a chance and then re-assess as you go. This is the process of growth: limited risk followed by learning followed by risk and so on.

The key to risk management is to approach everything with the understanding that risk is inherent. Your job is to evaluate the risk and trust that you have everything you need to deal with what you don't know. Returning to the startup example, you leave your job not because you are taking a huge risk but because you are confident that you have a good idea and know that you can handle anything that comes your way. You have *faith* in yourself and your abilities. The risk is built in to whatever you choose, you are simply choosing to do the thing that has the best payoff.

Which leads to rewards. There is a saying about how 'fortune favors the brave'. There is also a saying that says, 'no risk, no reward'. Both are true and speak to the benefits of risk. When you embrace risk and have faith in yourself then your actions become very powerful. Your mind and body fill the future with hopes and dreams rather than fears and worries. Keep in mind that everything great in the world started first with a thought, and your thoughts become more powerful when you focus them on one point.

The opposite of faith is worry. When you worry you waste your precious energy on unproductive mental chatter. Worry also creates inflated perceptions of risk, which then cause a negative feedback loop as everything in the world starts to look scary and risky. People who spend their time thinking about all the potentially bad things that can happen rarely produce *anything*. These people sit in their houses deluding themselves that they have minimized risk when in reality they are living the very disaster they hope to avoid: A life full of dread and unrealized dreams.

If you are worry about 'what might happen' then I encourage you to face those worries early and often. Look at your fearful thoughts and then take a conscious, small step in that direction in the face of those thoughts. Become comfortable with the uncertainties and embrace the fear within you. This is the definition of courage: To feel fear and take action anyway. There is an incredible exhilaration in the process of doing what you fear! And although it might feel like it, you are not going to die from 99.99% of the risks you take. It is more likely you have simply inflated the risks in order to not have to give up a current version of yourself. You will be OK. Your family will be OK. Your life will turn out fine. Trust all this and take a small step forward.

Life is short. I encourage you to live your life to the fullest extent possible. As the old saying goes, you will never lie on your death-bed regretting that you didn't work another day in that job you hate. You will, however, regret the dreams you never followed and the hopes you never realized. *The only risks that matter are those that drive you to live in a small version of yourself.* You can live a life of greatness if you are willing to give up your fears and doubts. Break away from your current life! Embrace the 'risks' that cause you to worry! You can be smart about risks and yet still dream big dreams. This is your duty as an entrepreneur.

Key Takeaways:

- Life itself is full of risks. You cannot avoid them.
- Inaction carries as much risk as action.
- Worrying about risks is a waste of time and energy.
- You cannot control the world, all you can do is learn from it.
- Overstating risk can cause you to give up your hopes and dreams.
- If you want to live in a bigger version of yourself you must risk giving up your current way of being.
- Rarely will a business risk kill you. You can evaluate legitimate risks, but never give up your dreams.
- If something scares you or you deem it 'risky', then take small steps in the face of what you fear. This can bring incredible exhilaration.
- Being an entrepreneur means doing new things, and there is always risk in 'newness'. Get comfortable with this.

Case 1: Lenny's lament

Lenny is an entrepreneur in his own mind. He has ideas almost daily and repeatedly points to new products that he 'thought of years earlier'. According to Lenny's brother Bruce, "Lenny is extremely creative and smart. He is constantly calling me with new concepts and ideas. The problem is he never does anything about them." At one point Bruce asked Lenny if he would ever consider starting a company to follow through on one of his ideas. He replied that he would if he did not have a family to support and a mortgage to pay. According to Lenny, "the single guys have it easy. I have a family. You don't realize what that means. I can't just go off and do things everyone else is free to do."

"Lenny has always used something or someone as his reason not to take the leap," Bruce reflected. "First it was his coursework in college, then the demands of his job, then his savings account balance, now his family. I worry that he is eventually going to start to resent his family for 'holding him back'. The simple truth is that Lenny has a job that he hates and is too scared to risk failing on his own." As of today Lenny is still in his job, grumbling about the work, and coming up with 'the next big thing'. Bruce summarizes that, "To Lenny, the risks in creating his own business are greater than the risks of staying in his current crappy and unfulfilled life. I feel for him, I really do."

Case 2: K.C.'s decision

In 1999 I was sitting very pretty in my role as a Senior Management Consultant at a large technology firm in Boston. In just one year I had brought in multiple large clients, was making a great salary (with options), and was being told that I could easily climb the corporate ranks. I felt like I had the world at my fingertipss and was very excited about the future.

Then one day I received a phone call from a friend who suggested I might make a good CTO for a new startup. The company was based in Boston and was at a very early stage. My conversations with the founders went well and, in a few weeks, I received an offer that included founding shares. The only sticking point was that they wanted me to join within a week...or else the offer was off the table. This was very stressful because the stock options at my firm were due to vest in 2 months. If I left today I was essentially leaving $300,000 on the table. I felt like I was risking a lot leaving that much money and potential on the table. My boss, my family and my friends all thought I would be crazy to go with an unknown company.

In the end I went with the startup, and was glad that I did. Shortly after leaving, my previous employer was hit hard in the crash of 2000. My options went underwater and would have been worthless. The company also laid off over 80% of the workforce, so even if I had been able to keep my job the prospects would have been dim. Our startup, by contrast, raised money and went on to be purchased five years later for $80 million. The road was difficult, to be sure, but it paid off handsomely.

I tell this story to all of my clients to emphasize that risk is only what you make of it. If you believe in yourself you can change almost any risk into an opportunity. Rather than worry about risks, spend your energy thinking about what you are going to create!

LESSON 16: TRANSPARENCY = TRUST

Transparency is one of the most controversial concepts in relationship psychology, but it is also one of the most powerful. Without it, people cannot trust each other. With it, you can build very effective and productive organizations. Transparency is at the heart of a powerful corporate culture and is the main reason behind the success or failure of personal relationships. Trust between people is directly correlated to the level of transparency involved. So what, exactly, is transparency?

Transparency is, in short, the degree to which people share their 'truth' with one another. When people are transparent they open up and share in a way that helps others understand what they think and who they are. They are able to connect with one another and trust that each person is capable of hearing the truth. This 'truth telling' eliminates mistrust because all the facts are present, nothing is hidden. When people know that the truth is being told they can relax and think rationally. On the other hand, when people suspect that something is hidden they live in a state of debilitating fear and doubt.

The reason transparency is so important can be found in our ancient history. Tens of thousands of years ago, when humans lived mainly in small tribal groups, there was quite a lot of fear and doubt. If you were walking through the woods and came upon a human that you did not know, your first instinct in this dog-eat-dog world would be to mistrust. You would be on high alert for hidden signs of mal-intent. Each movement, facial expression and sound would be evaluated so that you could understand if this person was a friend or foe. The more you knew, the better you could protect yourself.

Flash forward to today and we see how this instinct plays out. If someone hides something from us, we mistrust. If people are open and honest, we relax because we know the truth. Although we are not in life-or-death situations, we still feel as if we need to protect ourselves from potential harm. Cultures that are predicated on withholding information, skewing the truth and deceiving its members are considered 'toxic' because they degrade individuals through worry and doubt. Cultures that are based on honesty, openness and feedback are 'healthy' because the members know where they stand and relate to each other with trust.

All of this may seem fairly rational, but in reality it is quite controversial. Many people do not *want* to be transparent. For many of us transparency is a risk because it exposes us to the potentially harsh judgment of others, and we understandably don't want to be judged. Consider the woman having an affair or the man losing his paycheck on gambling. They don't tell 'their truth' because they fear what people will think of them, especially those close to them. They want to control their reality by manipulating what they say and don't say. It is not a moral wrong as much as an attempt to protect oneself from attack by another. For this reason many of us hide our truth, and in the process create distance from one another.

Telling the complete truth takes guts. It also takes work. In the workplace this means telling people exactly what you think and what you are doing. It means telling the truth about controversial subjects, even if it brings up fear. In order to have a trust-based organization every member must feel encouraged and allowed to talk about *anything*, especially the things that go unsaid. I know this feels crazy, but without it you cannot expect trust from the people on whom your success depends.

Now, this does not mean that every piece of information needs to be shared. You don't need to tell everyone about your personal issues, or even expose your ownership stake in your company. Information sharing does requires discretion. You do, however, need to share things that have an impact on others, especially in personal relationships. If you are thinking about moving the company, you must share this if you want to maintain the trust of the people around you. You must allow them the dignity of their response. If they want to quit, then so be it. You cannot control or manipulate how people respond to you, only what you say.

When sharing truth there are some ways that are more effective than others. I have seen some leaders interpret transparency as 'telling the hard truth' in a way that is painful and destructive. If you think, for example, that an employee is not doing well, you don't just walk up and say 'you suck'. You learn to communicate in a way that is safe (see Communication Lesson #13) and enables the listener to *hear* your truth, no matter how difficult. When you speak you do so with compassion, yet still with absolute truth. Doing this well results in not only trust between people but also a more complete and thorough transfer of information.

As an entrepreneur, I encourage you to practice transparency. Here are some things you can be transparent about:

1. State of the company. Be open about your company. Tell the truth about where you are and what you are doing. You don't need to tell your competitors what you are up to, but you do need to share what you are doing and thinking with your employees and investors. Manipulating information and lying will only destroy your culture over the long term.
2. State of your products. Tell your customers the truth about what you sell. Hiding shortcomings only delays the day of reckoning. Eventually customers find out the truth, and if you have skewed or 'spun' the information they will never forgive you. Be open and honest about what you sell.
3. Your thoughts. Trust the people around you. Open up to them...especially the members of your team. If you don't know something, admit it. Show trust in those on whom you

depend, and they will return that trust. If you are deceived, then you have learned something valuable about the relationship.

4. Your feelings. Emotions are the gateway to powerful actions. If you are angry or hurt, admit it. If you are happy, show it. When people feel your emotional transparency they will respond in kind. They will also trust that you are being 'real' with them, which will help them relax and focus on work.

There are many opportunities to create transparency, but two of the most powerful involve formal meetings. I recommend you regularly hold both one-on-one and group meetings where the explicit intent is to be transparent. In one-on-one meetings you need to be open about a person's performance, your intentions for the company, and your thoughts about anything that concerns that person. In return, you must also be willing to hear *anything* that person needs to say. It is your responsibility to *encourage* transparency through both words and deeds. If you make it OK, people will tell you the truth.

For most leaders, transparency is hardest during group meetings. I am always shocked at how poorly managers handle these meetings by either trying to tamp down dissent or by being shockingly or disrespectfully candid. It is possible, through practice, to have a group meeting where the truth is told (and heard) safely. This is your task: to learn how to create a space where people can share how they feel and what they think in safety, even if it causes consternation or conflict. Trust me, you would rather hear about a mutiny *before* it occurs, rather than being surprised by it because you were unwilling to hear hard truths!

If you decide to hide information, manipulate the truth or stop people from telling the truth, beware. Over time customers will stop doing business with you, regulators will pursue you, and your employees will come to despise you. Even if you think you are 'technically' telling the truth, you can be seen as manipulative and untrustworthy. Tell a customer that something works when it does not and see what happens over the long term. Likely you will not have very many customers. Tell an employee that things are fine when they are not, and they will eventually leave the company. The truth *always* finds a way to surface, so you want to be on the right side of information when it appears. When you were a kid, perhaps, you learned that it was better to tell your parents about your bad grades *before* they saw your report card. That way you could at least have a chance to explain yourself. As a business owner it is imperative that you become practiced at open and honest communication before you need to.

As mentioned in earlier chapters, listening is key to creating a transparent environment. When you listen well you create safety. By being open to hearing anything you tell the people around you that it is OK to be transparent. When people feel it is safe to share, they open up and tell you things you would never expect. You learn about dissent, you hear worries about product quality, and you get an inside track on new ideas. Transparency helps people relax and access their gifts. When you have a culture built on transparency then you have a foundation of trust, which is the key to cooperation and high performance.

Transparency also positively affects your life outside your company. When customers trust you they give you leeway and overlook your little mistakes. When your spouse trusts you, he/she can support you and help you be a more effective and successful person. Transparency is the currency of relationships, and relationships are the force behind highly successful entrepreneurs.

I strongly encourage you to develop transparency within yourself and in all aspects of your life. Hiding, skewing and manipulating the truth creates shame, and shame is draining. In the long term you will feel much freer and more effective if you can open yourself up to the world in a way that builds trust. There is a saying that 'perfect vulnerability equals perfect safety'. Once you allow yourself to be vulnerable in transparency you will find that people return the favor. Love, loyalty and close relationships are all the result of your willingness to be 'vulnerably transparent', so practice this skill with dedication!

Key Takeaways:

- Transparency is the willingness to share truth.
- Trust requires truth telling.
- When people trust each other they communicate openly and cooperate on joint tasks.

- When people do not trust each other they cannot work together.
- Shading or hiding the truth never works. Truth always surfaces.
- Your long-term success depends on your willingness to be personally and professionally transparent.
- The strength of your relationships and the 'okayness' of your internal state are determined by your level of transparency.
- In order to create an environment of transparency you must be willing to speak and hear anything without judgment

Case 1: Spin Doctor

Torrey is a great CEO and a brilliant entrepreneur. She can spot product trends, get financing, and push people to execute on their plans. Her employees often comment that she 'seems like a superhero'…with intellectual powers that verge on magical. What she also had, according to her partners, was a 'challenged relationship to the truth'. "Torrey used to get really worked up in meetings and start spinning stories about the state of our products," one team member recalled. "It was not that she was telling lies but more that she was inflating, sometimes dramatically, their capability. Our engineers got ulcers just listening to her!"

Over time Torrey's 'spinning' took a toll. In speaking with her employees, it was clear that they didn't trust a word that came out of her mouth. "There was a rampant rumor mill at our company," the HR manager confessed. "Nobody knew what was true or not, and so everyone tried to fill in the blanks with speculation. Torrey didn't really do anything to clarify what she said and tended to hold certain information close to the vest. The result was a team that doubted everything." Even worse, the customers had begun to question the legitimacy of the company. "Our market reputation was, frankly, shit," declared one exasperated business development executive. "Customers have said to my face that they don't believe a thing we say and that they simply don't want to do business with us because of all the spin."

Torrey was largely in denial until participating in a meeting with an unhappy customer. According to the customer, "We lit into her. We told her, to her face, that we did not trust a word she said and that we were considering suing her for fraud. We had paid her company over $1 million in fees and felt like we had been duped. When the product failed in our last usage she went right to the contract and told us she had been as upfront as the contract specified and that she was not liable. We were absolutely livid." In the end, the customer decided never to do business with Torrey's company again, while her employees whispered about the imminent death of the company.

Case 2: Spin Doctor (revisited)

After the disastrous customer meeting, Torrey was chastened. She approached her closest confidant, a co-founder, and asked for feedback. "Torrey came to me hat-in-hand," her friend recalled. "She had never been given such a public lashing. To her credit, she asked me for honest feedback, and I gave it to her." After this conversation Torrey decided to turn over a new leaf. She called a company meeting and declared that she was going to open up about everything, and asked her team to support her in being exact about her declarations. One of her employees recalled, "It was one of the bravest things I have ever seen. Torrey admitted everything and asked us to be honest with her. It took guts."

Over the next weeks Torrey talked to everyone in the company and got first-hand feedback. She told each person the truth about the company and its products while also listening very intently to what people said. "The turnaround was remarkable," her friend said. "Torrey became almost embarrassingly open about herself. She held nothing back...and it worked!" As part of her process Torrey hired an executive coach and assigned an internal 'culture manager'. The concept of transparency was introduced as a cultural value and embedded in all company interactions.

"Torrey even called all our customers and personally apologized," her business development leader told us. "She was very straightforward and open, and the customers responded. Although we certainly did not gain back all of the customers we lost, I feel like I can now at least talk to them with a straight face." Eventually Torrey's company came back from the brink and currently has a very strong and thriving business culture. Customers like her and her employees trust her. One employee summed it up well, "Now at least I know what we are doing and feel free to talk about my concerns. It is just so much more relaxing here than it used to be! I find I am proud of what we do and, well, I actually like coming to work now!"

LESSON 17: ALIGN YOUR TEAM

When you start a small company, the first thing you realize is that every person within your company has an impact on its direction. You, as the leader, have the most impact, but each individual can also add or take away from the energy you put toward what you are trying to accomplish. For this reason it is imperative that everyone working on your project have a very clear idea of what you are trying to do, how you intend to do it, and when everything needs to happen. Surprisingly even with small groups this is not always the case.

Every person who joins your company will have a unique perspective. They will look at the world in a different way than you, and this is generally good. Creativity and thorough performance are driven by diversity of opinion and skill. If everyone looked at things exactly the same way then the company would suffer from a very narrow mind and skill-set. I believe, in fact, that you must look for people who *don't* think the way you think in order to get the best range of opinions on a subject. A large aspect of good leadership involves coordinating competing opinions, thoughts and skill sets in order to maximize your responses to a highly dynamic market.

With the diversity of opinions, however, also comes misunderstanding. People who think the way you think will immediately 'get' what you are trying to do. People who do not have your same lens of the world will very likely miss your point if you are not clear enough about your vision and strategy. It is for this reason you must constantly over-communicate and seek to clarify your strategy, goals and vision. You cannot assume that your team is 'on board' with what you are doing. They very likely have a different understanding, sometimes extremely different.

As a leader, part of your job is to communicate the direction of your company both externally and internally. External communication involves investors, board members, customers and 'the market'. Communicating to external parties is easy for most CEOs because the need is obvious and pressing. Internal communication involves dialogue with managers and employees *within* the company. This type of communication, although extremely important, is in my experience the one most neglected by leadership.

If you are going to create an effective company you must treat every person as an important aspect of your culture, even those with whom you disagree. This becomes especially important if your company is small (less than 20 people). Each employee of a small company has contact with customers, investors and the community. Every person you hire can influence your direction in either a positive or negative way. It is imperative that you work with your team both individually and as a group to come up with a 'common language' about what you are doing, why you are doing it, and how you are going to get where you are going.

I call this process 'orienting the group', because it involves turning disparate views into a cohesive direction. Somewhat like 'herding cats', only these 'cats' are sentient and willful. You cannot force human beings to do what you say. You must listen, compromise, persuade and inspire in order get everyone going in the right direction. Visually, the process looks like this:

START:

FINISH:

The key to accomplishing this is, once again, skillful communication. When you speak about your vision you must do so clearly and with

passion. People need to be able to paint a vivid picture of what you are trying to build, and why you are building it. When you describe your goals you must also do so with specificity and knowledge. Your targets should be well researched and achievable. As you speak of the strategy for achieving your vision and goals you will need to speak of it in a way that clear, directional and leaves no room for ambiguity. In order for people to act they must completely understand the logic and meaning behind your thinking.

As if this were not enough, you must also be able to listen to feedback regarding your thoughts *while you are communicating.* Your fellow leaders and employees will have opinions, and you should be able to hear those opinions 'on the fly'. Many CEOs and founders make the mistake of talking in a way that does not allow for interjection or disagreement. They bowl their listeners over with bluster, confidence or force of will. In the worst cases leaders actively discourage feedback by 'slamming' those who offer a different perspective. When this happens people walk away feeling confused, discouraged and disheartened. If you want to be successful, this in *not* the way you want your partners and employees to feel.

Successful communication of vision, goals and strategy involves a very simple process:

1. **Prepare.** Think through how you want to talk about what you are trying to convey. Practice either in your own head or with a friend. Focus on being inspirational, persuasive and

very clear.

2. **Speak.** State your purpose for speaking, articulate your vision, and communicate what needs to be done. Speak with positive energy and a belief that your team can do anything. Inspire!

3. **Seek feedback.** Ask people to articulate what they have heard. Encourage them to ask questions and offer competing opinions.

4. **Listen.** Stay quiet and intensely focused on what you hear from people. Let them have a complete thought. Reflect what you are hearing back to the people in the room (i.e. 'if I hear you correctly, you are saying...') so that you can be sure you understand.

5. **Clarify and correct.** If someone has his or her facts wrong or misunderstands what you are saying, then carefully and kindly re-communicate what you want to say. Be patient. Take the time you need to make sure everyone understands. Repeat the listen/clarify process until everyone is clear.

This may seem like an unnecessarily burdensome process for a fast moving company, but in my experience it is absolutely necessary to avoid catastrophic miscommunication. Trust me, you would much rather dedicate a few hours up front ensuring everyone is 'on-board' than finding out halfway through the product cycle that the team misheard your intentions. Good communication not only helps you avoid extremely costly mistakes, but it also creates a sense of shared meaning and purpose that drives teams to success. As a leader it is imperative that you learn how to do this well. Your future in business depends on it!

Key Takeaways:

- In order to be successful you have to be good at communicating your vision, goals and strategy.
- Not everyone thinks the same way, nor do they hear the same things. Everyone has a 'lens' through which they perceive.
- Miscommunication is expensive and time consuming.
- Successful companies are those where the individuals work with a common purpose and direction.
- You must practice communicating effectively: Speak, ask, listen, repeat. Be sure your team understands what you are trying to say.
- Be patient with people. Let them misunderstand and disagree. They will be much more loyal if you let them have space to be different.
- Seek to inspire through positive energy. Be inspired!

Case 1: The Reluctant Engineer

The executive team of Axion Devices sat around the table looking at each other in confusion. Their CEO and founder, Roy, had just delivered another one of his diatribes about the latest product release. He was angry that certain functions were not included in the final spec and wanted somebody's head on a platter. "I swear that we had gotten it right," remembered Axion's chief engineer, "but Roy was yelling about how we had not listened to what he said." After Roy had calmed down, Axion's head of marketing asked him to clarify what, exactly, he had found lacking.

"After an hour of back and forth we figured out that there had been a horrible miscommunication," the head of marketing recalls. "Roy had been speaking with too many people and conveying messages that were not clear. In the end the team was forced to make assumptions about what they heard, and the result was a product that did not meet Roy's requirements. You would think that in a small company would would have gotten it right...yet this went on for over 6 months!" Seeing that there was a problem, the team suggested they hire a management consultant to come in and look at the situation. Reluctantly, Roy agreed.

"The consultant's findings were interesting, to say the least," according to Axion's head of HR. "She interviewed virtually everyone in the company and said that we had a systemic miscommunication issue. Because we are an engineering organization, and Roy is a brilliant engineer himself, there was a tendency to 'silo' ourselves into our own little worlds. And Roy, as a communicator, is not very good at articulating what he wants. So everyone walks away thinking they heard him correctly, but in reality nobody clearly understood the assumptions and targets."

As a result of the findings, the consultant was hired to facilitate a number of team meetings, during which she pointed out the many times where a statement or piece of information could be misinterpreted or misunderstood. "It was remarkable," said the HR director. "Roy was able to see the ambiguity of his words and learned to ask for confirmation. We found out that 90% of the time we were misinterpreting what Roy was trying to say! With practice, all of us got better at speaking and reflecting. Now we don't have anywhere near the problems we did before."

Case 2: Communication as a Process

Laura is the founder of a marketing firm whose employees and clients span the globe. "We decided from the outset that we were not going to have an office until we absolutely had to," Laura relayed. "Most of the founding team had families, and so we wanted to be able to work from home and manage our own schedules." Very soon after founding the company, however, Laura and the team experienced the downsides of a 'distributed model'. "Miscommunication was immediate and rampant," Laura remembers. "Team members were very busy and so were constantly texting or leaving messages for one another. Eventually a ball would get dropped and then accusations would fly. Because we were so infrequently together we had a hard time staying on the same page."

As a result, Laura instituted a formal communication schedule and process. Each week the team gathered on the phone to talk about the direction of the company and the priorities of goals. On these calls Laura required that everyone adhere to a process of 1) speaking, 2) asking for specific help if necessary, 3) asking the listeners to repeat what they heard and 4) clarifying or confirming the initial statement. The speaker would then give an overview and ask for formal confirmation from each person. "It was a bit of a pain in the ass at first," Laura recalls. "But very quickly it became habitual. We got really good at communicating."

As a byproduct of the process, Laura was able to stretch her team's ability to perform. "Even though we were not in the same room we became really good at motivating each other," Laura shared. "There was a lot of laughter and camaraderie on the phone. Once the misunderstandings and confusion were eliminated, we were able to have more fun with our work." Today Laura's company is growing very rapidly and the distributed model has proven to be an asset. "It is really easy to recruit people now because we can get them from anywhere," Laura says happily. "Everyone is self-motivated and yet constantly in touch. We have twice-yearly off-sites so we can see each other personally, but most of our interactions are phone based. Everyone feels very close because our communication is so good!"

LESSON 18: CREATE ALTERNATIVES AND OPTIONS

In the book <u>Getting to Yes</u>, William Fisher and Robert Ury teach the reader to establish a 'BATNA', or 'best alternative to a negotiated agreement', in every negotiation. Put simply, a BATNA is a backup plan that gives you options if the negotiation does not work out. A BATNA keeps you from agreeing to things that do not suit you, and it also keeps the person across the table from using a lack of options as a potential weakness. If you have no other option, you are inherently in a weak position. A BATNA puts you in a more powerful position because you have less fear of walking away.

This concept extends to virtually everything in business, and especially so in the start-up world. When you start a company you are in an inherently weak position. You have no company, no product and sometimes no money. There is no brand equity to fall back upon because your name is unknown. When coaching entrepreneurs the people I find most challenging are former executives from large companies, mainly because they have taken for granted the brand value of their previous positions and are unprepared for the rejection they receive when starting out on their own. Their power to negotiate and cut deals goes from strong to virtually nil, and it freaks them out.

When you are in a relatively weak position in regards to potential investors, suppliers, customers or partners, is it imperative that you create alternatives whenever you enter into a negotiation. Each of these market players will, if permitted, gladly take advantage of your weakness if he/she thinks they can get move the price or terms in his/her favor. Here is how it works for each:

- **Investors**. When you talk to investors they will almost always ask you a) how much cash you have in the bank and b) who else you are talking to. These questions, among others, should be seen as the beginning of the negotiation, not just information gathering. If you are not talking to anyone else and don't have much money in the bank, then your position is very weak and they will seek to get more of your company. You should always have at least 6 months of cash 'runway' and a list of potential investors on your appointment calendar (ideally interested investors). You also want to move very quickly, because every day you burn more cash and put yourself at greater risk.
- **Suppliers**. Whatever company you are trying to start, you will have suppliers. If you are a service company then it may

simply be office space, supplies and people. If you are a product company then you will have raw materials and parts. In either case, when a supplier knows that you have only one purchasing option (s)he will use his/her power to negotiate terms. Because of this, you should *always* interview multiple providers in order that you get the best arrangement and send the message that one supplier cannot hold you over a barrel. If it happens that there is only one supplier for what you require then come up with alternative processes or methods that are plausible work-arounds. Whomever you are talking to should know from the outset that you have alternatives (this applies to hiring as well).

- **Customers**. When you are starting a company you have no product and therefore no customers. Potential buyers know this and it both scares them and offers them an opportunity. Because you are new some customers might be nervous to buy your offering, yet early adopters might also see an opportunity to get more favorable terms. For these reasons you want to start each conversation by listing all the people who are interested in buying what you have. You must build 'social proof' of both your product's acceptance and your options for selling. When people know others are buying what you have, they are not only reassured, but they are also more likely to accept your price and terms.

- **Partners**. Everyone wants to associate with a winner. When you look for a partner (either a person or a company), you will want to know that (s)he is headed in a positive direction and will be a net asset to your business. (S)he is evaluating you in the same way. When you talk to potential partners you want to have multiple companies and people in the background with whom you are having the same conversations. Create networks in your industry such that you have many supporters and possible alliances. The more people see you as a 'mover and shaker', the more likely it will be that they will want to work with and for you.

When you create alternatives you are creating confidence, and when you have confidence you send the message that you have what it takes to be successful. People are attracted to those who exude success, and repelled by any whiff of failure. Make yourself attractive! Before every meeting 'pump yourself up' with lists of people who are trying to help you and have spoken with you. This process has a similar benefit as working on a business plan: The more groundwork you do, the more confident and knowledgeable you will appear.

Another version of a BATNA (except in reverse) is what is called a 'horserace'. A horserace occurs when there are multiple bidders interested in a limited commodity. For example, if you have 20 investors interested in the 3 slots you have for investment, then you have a horserace. Those investors will fight to win the opportunity to invest with you. This scenario allows you to dictate the terms because you have multiple BATNAs with each investor. You negotiate with confidence knowing that you have many people interested in what you have.

Most people find themselves surprised and pleased when a horserace occurs, but in reality you don't have to rely on fate. You can *create one* yourself. Simply seek out potential buyers and encourage them to see the value that all of the other potential buyers have seen. It is somewhat like dating. When two or more people are interested in dating you it is much more likely that others will wonder what they are missing! They will want what you have. People get envious when they think they are going to miss out on something valuable. If you have one person interested in buying your company then find 2 others who may be interested as well. Let them fight each other for you. If possible, NEVER let there be only one bidder for what you are selling.

Before I close this lesson, a warning: As you go about the process of creating alternatives and horseraces you are likely going to be tempted by the two deal killers 'hubris' and 'deceit'. Hubris is the arrogance that sometimes comes with alternatives. When you are on top of the world and know you have many people interested, you are more likely to treat others badly. Your confidence can slowly morph into mean-ness, which can drive people to be spiteful and irrational. I have seen situations in which a CEO has gone from having 3-4 interested parties in a negotiation one moment to having *none* the next, simply because his arrogance and over-confidence pissed off the bidders.

The other deal killer, deceit, occurs when you are so hungry to be seen as powerful that you lie about what you have. For example, you may be tempted to invent fictitious investors or overstate a potential investor's interest in your company. This is understandable, especially if you are feeling insecure. I know the feeling of walking into that first meeting with no money and no prospects…it stinks. Yet I also encourage you to be truthful about yourself and your progress. If you are just starting out, say so…but also say that you have 5 meetings lined up right after (and make sure you do!). It will be tempting to lie, spin or deceive. Don't do it! You will be caught eventually and, when you are, people will stay away from you like you have a contagious disease. Be truthful but confident, and follow up your confidence with *action*.

Leaders who are good at creating alternatives create something called 'option value'. Option value is a financial term that describes the monetary value of instruments designed to hedge certain investments. If you have an investment in one commodity, for example, and an 'option' to buy that same commodity at a different price sometime in the future, then you have hedged your initial investment. Investors use options to counter the risks of price fluctuations in their underlying investments. With options they create a more stable price scenario and minimize their risk of catastrophic loss. After much study academics figured out that these options were not only smart investments, but that they also had monetary value in-and-by themselves. Thus 'option value'.

The point of option value is that when you create alternatives and options in your business dealings you are *actually creating financial assets*. Your alternatives are *worth something*. If you were mathematically inclined you could likely calculate the monetary value of some of your options, although I don't recommend you wasting your time. Just trust me when I say that options and alternatives have more than conceptual value. When you create a BATNA and/or a horserace you not only increase your confidence and likelihood of closing a deal, you also increase the asset value of your firm. In every scenario, be it hiring, negotiating or selling, always create alternatives and options. Learning to do this is a key entrepreneurial skill.

Key Takeaways:

- Create alternatives and options for every business situation.
- When you have alternatives, you have confidence. Confidence gives you power.
- Your options have value. If you want to increase the value of your company, increase your options.
- Create a BATNA for every negotiation.
- When selling, have other buyers. When buying, have other sellers.
- Always have/create a horserace when selling a limited commodity.
- Be kind and considerate in all business dealings. Avoid arrogance.
- Tell the truth positively and confidently. Never lie!

Case 1: Investor Madness

Toni was exasperated as she hung up the phone. "I don't know what in the world is going on!" she exclaimed. Just three months ago she had come across an investor who positively gushed about her startup. "He seemed very excited about what we're doing. I was relieved that we finally had someone seriously interested," Toni recalled. "It felt good to get back to working on our prototype rather than spending all our time fundraising." As the months wore on, however, nothing seemed to move forward with the investor. Each meeting concluded with more confusing messages and terms.

"We were very trusting," Toni relates. "We thought for sure that this guy was our savior. So we just kept working and assumed the best. Now I'm not so sure." Now, three months after the first meeting, Toni's company was running low on cash. "Our 'savior' has started sending strange messages," Toni told us. "He's now talking about the 'weak market' for our product and how risky the startup world is. He is either getting cold feet or negotiating...I'm just not sure. The problem is that now we don't have many other options. We only have about 1 month of cash left, and seeking other investors would kill our product development. I am super stressed out!"

Case 2: Investor Jackpot

It was early 2000, and the investor world was rumbling. The market was 'irrationally exuberant' and a crash was imminent. Steve knew they had to move fast to raise money for his new startup. "I wanted to have an investment round closed in 30-60 days because I knew the window was about to close," Steve remembers. So the 3 members of the founding team gathered their prototypes and presentations and hit the road. "We had organized over 20 pitch meetings with venture firms from around the country. We went at it hard. And it was a risk because we had so much we needed to do," Steve related.

The first few meetings were non-committal but gave the team a sense of purpose and momentum. Steve later said, "We got better and better at our pitch, and were able to refer to previous meetings in future discussions. We gave each VC an impression of momentum and clear direction. Every time they asked, we said we had plenty of money in the bank and that we had many serious names interested in investing. I told them that the book was filling up and you'll want to be a part of this. And it worked!" When the team returned they hit the phones and emphasized the deadline to invest. "We refused to let them string us along," Steve said. "We created a horserace, a deadline, and then pushed the round to a close."

Steve ended up closing on the day the market tanked. "Literally, on the day of the crash there were term sheets streaming off the fax machine," Steve remembers. "I was on the phone telling the investors they were out if they did not send a term sheet and cash immediately. We were really sweating it." Steve and his team had initially wanted to raise $15 million for their first major round of funding, yet ended up bringing in over $30 million by the time the deadline closed. "It was incredible," Steve laughed. "We raised enough money to take our company through the downturn and went on to become the star player in our market. It was a textbook investment round."

LESSON 19: WATCH YOUR CAP TABLE

One of the most important spreadsheets, and one of the least understood by entrepreneurs, is called a 'Cap Table'. A Cap Table is short for Capitalization Table. It indicates the number of shares owned by each shareholder, including the percentage ownership that his/her shares represent. This document is important because certain classes of stock have voting rights, so knowing who owns how many of those shares will tell you who controls the company. When someone, or a group of people, have control of your company they can do all sorts of things like issue shares, set policy, choose a new direction, or fire key executives like…you.

When you create your company you (or you and your co-founders) will initially have 100% of the ownership. You will control the company because you have 100% of the votes. There are no other outside parties to challenge your control because you, as of yet, have no investors. To illustrate this better, let's take a simple example. Say you are a team of 3 founders starting a company. Your initial percentage ownership might look like this:

Shareholder	Shares	% Owned	
Founder 1	5,500,000	55.00%	
Founder 2	2,000,000	20.00%	100%
Founder 3	2,500,000	25.00%	
	10,000,000	100%	

At this stage Founder 1 (you) controls the company because you own over 51% of the voting shares, and with your founding team you own 100%. This will change as you raise capital (money), but for now you are secure.

Then let's say you seek investors to expand your business. This is called your first 'round' of investment. These initial rounds are called the 'Angel rounds' or 'Seed Rounds' because anyone who invests at this early stage (and at such high risk) is an angel from heaven! In this case I have chosen what I call 'Early Angels', such as friends and family (which is common because at this stage they are the only people who will invest and not ask too many questions). In this example, you choose to sell these Early Angels 1,000,000 shares. Your Cap Table now looks like this:

Shareholder	Shares	% Owned	
Founder 1	5,500,000	50.00%	
Founder 2	2,000,000	18.00%	91%
Founder 3	2,500,000	23.00%	
Early Angel 1	500,000	4.50%	
Early Angel 2	500,000	4.50%	
	11,000,000	100%	

You and your founding team have been 'diluted' in that your cumulative percentage ownership of the company has dropped from 100% to 91%. Founder 1 (you) still has control, but you no longer have *total* control because you do not own 51%. Theoretically Founders 2 and 3 could band together with the Early Angels to thwart your wishes because together they also own 50%. This is unlikely to happen if you trust your fellow founders and Angels, but it is technically possible given the voting percentages.

The Early Angel money you have raised will last you for a while, but then you may decide to get more investment. You put together a presentation and go out to external parties (given that you have tapped out your friends and family) and seek a formal 'Angel round'. In this example you find three Angels willing to buy a total of 1,080,000 new shares of the company at your now-increased price (the price of your shares will increase over time as you increase the value of the company, so the percentage you sell will be smaller and smaller per given dollar. For more information, see my book "Fund Your Dreams"). Your Cap Table has then changed to:

Shareholder	Shares	% Owned	
Founder 1	5,500,000	45.68%	
Founder 2	2,000,000	16.61%	83%
Founder 3	2,500,000	20.76%	
Early Angel 1	500,000	4.15%	
Early Angel 2	500,000	4.15%	
Angel 1	400,000	3.32%	
Angel 2	400,000	3.32%	
Angel 3	240,000	1.99%	
	12,040,000	100%	

You and the founding team have been diluted to 83%, and the Angels now own 17% collectively. Founder 1 (you) no longer has 51% and so you must rely on the other founders to keep voting control. As you can see, the more investors you include, the more you are at risk of losing control...especially when you start working with the 'sharks' like Venture Capitalists (VC's).

Let's now jump to the VC round or Series A. You are at the point where you want to raise a lot of money, say $5 million, to undergo major expansion. You find two VC's willing to buy 3,500,000 shares each (I am simplifying for this example. Usually one VC would buy more shares than the others and act as a 'lead' investor). Your Cap Table now is starting to look a bit dicey:

Shareholder	Shares	% Owned	
Founder 1	5,500,000	28.89%	
Founder 2	2,000,000	10.50%	52%
Founder 3	2,500,000	13.13%	
Early Angel 1	500,000	2.63%	
Early Angel 2	500,000	2.63%	
Angel 1	400,000	2.10%	
Angel 2	400,000	2.10%	
Angel 3	240,000	1.26%	
VC 1	3,500,000	18.38%	
VC 2	3,500,000	18.38%	
	19,040,000	100.00%	

You and your co-founders now own only 52% of the company. You are hanging on to control by your fingernails; one more investment round and you will lose voting control. Even in this round you are on thin ice because any of the investors could contact the others and try to band together to take control of the company. For example, some VC's have been known to contact other founders and convince them to vote against the CEO in exchange for promises (like the CEO role or cash awards). This is perfectly legal and very common. It is important for you to be aware of all the voting possibilities.

Numerically the concept of control is quite obvious and simple, but in reality it is very complex and nuanced. Investors are human beings and consequently can be unpredictable. Your job as founder and CEO is to constantly talk to your investors to 'take their temperature' and try to understand their motivations. You need to know if anyone is unhappy so you can address issues before they become a voting problem. You also need to find out if anyone is scheming against you to try to put together a voting block that can influence decisions. As the leader of the company one of your key roles is to keep an eye on your Cap Table and be very aware of where you stand.

If this sounds to you like politics, you are right. When you gather a group of strong-minded people together and give them an interest in an outcome then they will use their power to get what they want. This is human nature, to some extent. Yet many entrepreneurs ignore this truth and avoid dealing with their own political environment…to disastrous consequences. If you don't understand and manage your political environment then you are going to be a victim of whatever outcomes it generates.

Before I close this lesson, I want to offer a few other helpful suggestions. First, you must understand basic corporate structures.

Do your homework. Know the difference between C-Corps, S-Corps and LLC's. Choose wisely. Second, learn how governance works in each type of organization. In a C-Corp, for example, the board controls the company but investors have a vote as to who sits on the board. You want to know and trust your board, so try to get investors to vote for your choices. Last, get to know the different types of shares. In this lesson I assumed all shares are common stock with basic 1-share-1-vote rights. But in C-Corps you can have different classes of shares, each with different voting and participation agreements. You can, for instance, sell some investors non-voting shares, or others 2-1 voting rights. VC's are constantly trying increase their influence through these specialized agreements.

In summation, you need to be smart about investors and your Cap Table. Professional investors, like VC's, do this for living. They know how to craft share agreements such that they maximize their ownership rights and their potential for control. I have seen many, many entrepreneurs blindly accept an investor's terms simply because they were either too ignorant or too desperate to care. *Don't be one of those entrepreneurs.* Learn, seek advice, and pay attention to your Cap Table. Your job, and your company, literally depend on it.

Key Takeaways:

- Your Cap Table shows you who owns what percentage of your company.
- Anyone (or a group) who owns 51% or more of your voting shares 'controls' your company.

- You and your founders want to maintain control for as long as possible.
- With each round of investment you will give up a percentage ownership in the company. You will be 'diluted' and have less voting power.
- If a group of investors gains control, they can do anything they want with the company. It is *their* company.
- You must constantly pay attention to the Cap Table to see where you stand.
- You must also constantly communicate with your investors and board to make sure you understand where everyone else stands.
- Be smart. Learn about corporations and their governance. Don't leave it to lawyers. YOU must know and manage your own corporate structure.

Case 1: Locked Out

Jason paced outside the front door of his startup and fumed. His card-key no longer worked, and he could not get anyone on the phone. "What is going on!?" he ranted to himself. Slowly it occurred to Jason that this might have something to do with his recent tiff with the board. He knew that they were angry with him...but locking him out? No! There was no way they would throw out the founder of the company! He built this enterprise from the ground up! Sure they were having problems, but generally the company was doing well, wasn't it? The board was a mix of his and his VC's chosen representatives...would they have gotten together to oust him?

A year ago Jason had closed a large round of funding for his tech startup. During the process a banker friend had advised him that this round would dilute him to less than 35% ownership, putting Jason at risk of losing control. Jason had family who had also invested, which got him close to 50%, but he was aware that even with their cooperation he could not vote out members of the board. During the negotiations the lead VC had insisted that they get 2 members on the 3-person board. That made 5: Jason, his co-founder, an independent advisor, and the two VC's choices. Would his co-founder or the independent advisor turn on him? Jason did not want to believe what his gut was telling him.

In the end it turned out that the VC's had gotten together with Jason's co-founder and offered him the CEO position if he voted to oust Jason. The VC's did not believe in the direction Jason was taking the company and were tired of his threats and emotional histrionics. Jason related later that, "I guess I threw one too many fits. I really believed that as founder I had certain rights. I never thought they would just dump me. It was one of the most painful business realizations of my life. I now sit as a tiny shareholder in a company I started in my own apartment. It is humiliating." Jason started his company with 65% of the shares, but after multiple rounds of investment and financial restructuring was left with 2% of the common shares...and no job.

Case 2: Political Maneuvering

The Board of Directors loved Susan's leadership. She was CEO of a rapidly growing company that was poised to go public in a year or two, and had a great relationship with her team, the customers and the board itself. As one board member remembered, "Susan is incredibly good with people. She was constantly in touch with us during all phases of the company and always kept us in the loop. Even the VC-friendly representatives were taken by her!" Even though Susan had long ago lost her founder's majority, she was very aware of the political dynamics behind the board's decisions and managed them accordingly.

"I was very aware of who-owned-what shares and how many votes everyone had," Susan said. "We had 3 different investment rounds with different share agreements and rights. Each VC had negotiated special terms for their round that played into how they voted. I knew that in order to manage the board I would have to understand each person's position based on their underlying ownership interests." In order to keep the board on her side Susan made a habit of calling each board member once a month in order to discuss upcoming votes and initiatives. She also regularly called each investor and listened to their concerns, while at the same time updating them on progress. "I never assumed everything was OK," Susan told us. "I checked in constantly and let them know I was interested in their opinions. It made a huge difference."

Susan was also aware that she if she wanted the board to agree with her, she was going to have to get to them before they came up with their own ideas. According to Susan, "A lot of leaders will wait until the board meeting and then make their case for what they want to do. This is a mistake. By the time the meeting starts, many of the board members and investors have already had conversations and set up their positions. The board meeting is just a vehicle for voting." As a consequence, Susan made sure that she talked to each board member before the vote so that she could understand their positions and get their agreement. "I have never conducted a vote where I did not already know the outcome," Susan flatly stated. "I know I sound like a politician saying that, but it is the only way to get 7 people to give you what you want. I never, ever want to be surprised in a boardroom."

K.C. HILDRETH

LESSON 20: BECOME AN INSPIRATIONAL LEADER

When starting a company it is not enough to simply become a 'leader'. Average, run-of-the-mill leadership is fine for people running an existing organization or, for that matter, running the country. It is much easier to guide and encourage people when an organizational structure is already known. *Creating* a movement or an organization, however, requires something more…it requires *inspirational* leadership, and only you can provide this.

The word 'inspire' comes from the Latin 'inspirare', which means to 'inflame' or 'breathe into'. Later, in Old English, when someone was 'inspired' it meant that they had fallen under the 'immediate influence of God or a god'. I love these two definitions because, taken together, they define 'inspiration' as 'breathing the life of God into' something or someone. When you lead in an inspirational way you 'breathe the life of God' into those around you. To inspire someone is to help them access their own divine 'Spirit' (also derived from 'spirare', or 'breathe') in a way that moves, motivates and energizes. If you want to create something amazing you must be able to breathe Spirit into those around you. You must become an inspirational leader.

In truth, inspiration is much more about feeling than thinking. Consider this: Your conscious mind, the thinking part of your brain, is only about 5% of your mental processing power. The other 95% is subconscious. Further, your brain is only one part of a larger system that creates your experience of reality. Your heart and your gut, for example, have more nerve endings than your brain has neurons. Through your body you are constantly 'feeling the vibe' of the world around you and, if you listen to it, you can gain valuable guidance as to what is good or bad for you. In the system called 'You', your thinking mind is a bit player. Your body and subconscious mind are doing all the heaving lifting in the background, and doing so in a non-linear way that is much more complex and powerful than your chattering thoughts.

When you inspire someone, then, you are speaking to the 'non-thinking' part of them that is moved more by emotions than concepts. Facts and figures can never generate excitement in the way that hopes and dreams do. Churchill did not use wall-charts to galvanize the English people…he spoke of destiny, purpose and self-preservation. Gandhi didn't excite the Indian masses with a strong business case. He appealed to their higher selves and the hope of a better future. Martin Luther King Jr. did not change the country by lecturing on the importance of morality. He spoke emotionally to the part of us that knew what was right and good in the world. Inspirational leaders use *emotion* to convey their ideas because they know intuitively that it works. When people are *inspired* they can help a leader do incredible things (and, as in the case of people like Hitler, also do horrific things).

Inspirational leadership requires responsibility because it is so powerful. When you are good at inspiring an individual or group you can get them to do almost anything. Emotion is so powerful that it will trump the puny 'thinking mind' in almost every circumstance. If you want to raise money for your venture, inspire your investors. Once inspired, they will many times look past the 'facts' and go with their 'gut'. The same is true with future partners, employees and customers. People *want* to be inspired! They want to have the 'breath of God' inside of them. Your job is to learn how to do this in a way that is true and transparent for you.

It is very difficult to teach inspirational leadership because it is something that comes from *within* you. Your *soul* is the source of your inspiration. I can only show you the triggers that open you to your own divinity. The beauty of a truly inspirational leader is that (s)he doesn't really do anything in particular…(s)he simply accesses that part of them that is inspired and then shows it to the world. The world, in turn, responds. Inspired music moves the audience, inspired speech motivates action, inspired actions create followers. As Gandhi said, you must *be* the change you want to be in the world, and so it is true of the inspirational leader. You must *be inspired* in order to inspire others. The 'breath of God' must be in you before you can breathe it into others.

Here are some things you can do to inspire yourself so that you can then inspire those around you:

Believe. Throughout history inspirational leaders have used a deep reservoir of belief or faith to energize their actions. In some cases the belief is rooted in religious foundations, in others it is a love of country, and in still others it is a deep sense of what is good and right. In essence, every great leader has identified the 'why' behind what (s)he is doing, and this 'why' is deeply rooted in his/her belief about the world. In order to become and inspirational person you must claim what you believe and tell others your 'why' story. Without deep belief your ideas are merely transactional, with belief they become meaningful. Ask yourself: Why are you doing what you are doing? What is the higher good? Why should people care? Why are you the right person to do this? Answer these questions with confidence and *belief*. Believe in your mission, your goals, your impact and, most of all, *yourself*. Speak with the authority of someone who is convinced that (s)he is right…without hesitation or doubt.

Commit. There is a quote by W.H. Murray that speaks wonderfully to the power of commitment:

"Until one is committed,
there is hesitancy
The chance to draw back.

Always ineffectiveness.
Concerning all acts of initiative
there is one elementary truth,
the ignorance of which kills
countless ideas and splendid plans;
The moment one definitely commits oneself
then Providence moves too.
All sorts of things occur to help one
that would otherwise never occur.
A whole stream of events
issues from the decision,
raising in ones favor
all manner of incidents and meetings
and material assistance
which no person would have had come their way.
Whatever you think you can do
or believe you can do,
begin it now.
Action has magic, grace and power in it."

When you commit to something you *make a decision* to throw your entire being behind it. You 'burn the boats' and accept that your path will be forever changed. True commitment does not allow for half-measures, it is a total surrender to your decision. Giving yourself completely to that which you believe is inherently inspirational. When people see your absolute dedication to your craft, your business, and yourself, they will, even if they don't like you, be moved by your actions. 'Providence' will move to help you. Without total commitment your potential investors, employees, partners and customers will hesitate…simply because YOU are hesitating! If you want to inspire those around you, quit your job, turn over your savings, and throw your complete being into what you are trying to do. There is no other way.

Lead by example. For a number of years I have participated in the Big Brothers/Big Sisters mentoring program (among others). During my time with my little brother and in the course of many training programs, I learned that kids don't need to be told what to do, they need to be *shown who to be*. Children learn by *watching adults*. When what children see does not match what they hear, then they lose faith that the world is a trustworthy place. Kids want to see how you *are* in the world so they can model their own adult self. This 'observational method' of learning continues into adulthood. The people around you are watching you to see how you *act*, not what you say. For most people talk is indeed cheap. When who you are does not match what you say, then those around you will lose faith in you. When you act consistently with your ideals then people begin to trust you, and when they trust you they will follow you.

Lead by example in everything. Be willing to do the hard things that others don't want to do. Humble yourself. Speak difficult truths with kindness and compassion. Take responsibility for what goes wrong, and seek to make it right. Protect others. Stand in the front and 'take the bullets' for your team. Work hard and without complaint. *Act how you want others to act.* If you want others to be inspired by you then your deeds must loudly proclaim, "Follow me!"

Speak from the heart. The best way to inspire someone is to speak with emotional intensity. If you listen to the greatest speakers of all time they do not drone on about facts and figures…they speak with intensity and *emotion*. Truly inspirational people speak about things that matter to them. They talk about *truth* and *hope* and *love* and *greatness*. Inspirational speeches contain emotional words backed by emotional energy. So if you want to move a person or group of people then speak from your heart. Find something about your endeavor that is exciting and inspirational and focus on that. Seek meaning in what you are doing and then convey that meaning with energy and passion. When you do this you will kindle excitement in your listeners and help them access their own Spirit.

Learning to speak from your heart takes practice. Identify something in which you deeply believe – anything - and practice talking about it. Feel the warmth in your chest as you get into your topic. Smile, move your body, invite others into your expression! Talk about the things that matter to you, and why you find them so compelling. Be open and vulnerable. Express emotion easily. As you do these things you will see your audience resonate with your energy. They will move with you and open themselves to your leadership. This is the power of inspiration!

Connect with people. In order to be successful you must have smart people around you who are willing to work toward your goals. The only way to get these people to help you is to build relationships based on trust and understanding. When you create strong relationships you build connections that allow you to communicate and cooperate toward shared objectives. Connections happen when you do two things: Speak openly and honestly (and with kindness), and listen carefully and patiently. Speaking honestly builds trust, while listening carefully builds understanding. With trust and understanding you can inspire much more easily than if you have mistrust and confusion. People will never be inspired by leaders they don't trust, and will never follow someone who does not deeply understand their needs.

Your job is to connect with those around you, even those you don't like. Get to know them. Spend time trying to understand their motivations and interests. Remember their names! It may seem that this is a waste of time in your 'doing' world, but I can assure you it is not. When you spend time connecting with others, you build a loyal and dedicated following who will be open to your inspirational energy. You must create these connections if you want to create something great.

Stay positive. Emotional energy is inspiring, but it can also be destructive. Anger and hate can 'inspire' someone to do incredibly painful things. Hitler 'inspired' the German people to kill over 3,000,000 people. Negative emotional energy inspires because it taps into the fear response built into our biology. When any animal feels fear it responds instantly, and humans are no different. Thus political leaders are tempted to use negativity to motivate and 'inspire' the populace against anyone who disagrees with them. The problem with this approach is that negativity is inherently draining and destructive. People who use anger, hate or fear to get what they want inevitably destroy themselves in the process. Gandhi said:

"When I despair I remember that all through history the way of truth and love has always won. There have been tyrants and murderers and for a time they can seem invincible, but in the end they always fall. Think of it. Always."

If you want to create something lasting and powerful, you must focus on being a *positive* inspiration. Your entire being should exude joy and laughter. You must embody kindness and compassion. Your actions need to be consistent and loving. Positive inspiration can sometimes take a bit longer, but it tends to be long-lasting in its result. Negative sentiments, on the other hand, create a burst of energy, but it consumes itself in the process. So be an uplifting person. Love and encourage everyone around you. This one thing, by itself, can inspire others to greatness.

Work. Nothing demotivates and deflates a team more than a leader who does not work. This does not mean that you have to kill yourself (I have seen many leaders make this mistake), but it does mean that you need to execute on your tasks, follow through on your commitments, and do the things you are uncomfortable doing. Action always speaks louder than words, so follow your inspirational messages with concrete, productive activities. Walk the walk. Do your work. Help others do their work. Seek to be a leader that clears hurdles so that others can be successful. Put your back into it! The sight of a leader working side-by-side with those (s)he leads is highly inspirational. Every great leader in history was keen to walk with their people when the going gets rough. As much as you need to 'be' – in your kindness, your listening and your speech – you also need to 'do' to show others that you are not above getting your hands dirty.

Inspirational leadership is extraordinarily powerful because it can move people to stretch their own boundaries to achieve things that seem, at first blush, impossible. Great leaders inspire great outcomes. All major human movements and creations were inspired by someone, or a small group of people, with inspirational leadership skills. The success of your company will largely be determined by your ability to inspire and move others toward your vision. Although failure can be attributed to many causes, the primary driver behind an unsuccessful business is an unsuccessful leader.

Take responsibility for your role in leading your start-up. Inspire yourself and others to be GREAT. Aim high and never, ever give up.

Key Takeaways:

- Inspiration is a feeling. It is the 'breath of God' within you. Your Spirit.
- When you inspire yourself you become very powerful and energized.
- Inspiration comes when you believe something deeply and are working consistently with your beliefs.
- To cultivate your own inspiration you must believe in something, commit to it, and then exemplify that in your work.

- Inspirational leadership is when you transfer your inspiration to other people.
- When people are inspired they can do amazing things to help you.
- Inspirational leaders can literally change the world.
- If you want to be successful, learn to be inspirational!

Case 1: The Technocrat

Ron is a very smart guy with all the requisite degrees. Undergraduate from Yale and an MBA and JD from Harvard. Aside from the degrees Ron is also a very intense and rigorous thinker who can argue circles around even the best debater. "I have known Ron for many years," a business associate shared. "I have never met a smarter person. He can literally intimidate anyone intellectually. I have never won an argument with him...ever." The challenge for Ron was that his intelligence was off-putting. According to his associate, "There is an old saying that 'you can be right and still be wrong', and Ron embodied this. He was so smart that people left the room feeling insulted or deflated."

After working for a consultancy for a few years, Ron decided he wanted to start his own company. He wrote a brilliant business plan, brought on a partner, and raised initial funds from his friends and family. "We all thought Ron was going to be a billionaire," a friend remembered. "He was the kind of guy that just did not fail." As Ron went out to raise money and hire employees, however, his style began to affect the people around him. A former employee recalls that, "Ron was not fun to work with. He was so technical and intense that we all rolled our eyes when he spoke. Sure, he knew what he was talking about, but nobody liked being around him."

As time wore on, Ron increasingly alienated his investors and employees. The former employee continued, "Ron drove everyone away because he could not relate to them. He felt he was right and everyone, including the investors, were wrong. I don't think I ever remember Ron speaking to us in a way that would get us excited either. He just talked about how his way was best and that nobody understood. It was a deflating experience to work for him." In the end Ron's company sold for a modest amount, but to this day he has a challenge getting people to work for him or invest in his ideas. "Ron is just not an inspirational person," his associate sighs. "He is a technocrat stuck in a cycle of right and wrong. It's too bad, because the guy really does know what he is talking about." As of today Ron is back working for a consultancy, doing well in an industry that values his approach.

Case 2: The Visionary

The audience was mesmerized. As Tom paced around the room he talked about destiny and markets and the thrill of being part of the future. His new technology promised, in his words, to 'change the way people lived'. "I was completely taken," one of his former investors confided. "I was not sure of his idea, but Tom himself was one of the most powerful speakers I have ever heard. All of us were completely swept up by his passion and energy." And to be sure, Tom believed what he was saying. According to the investor, "Tom wasn't bullshitting us. He really thought – no he knew – that he had the next great invention. Unfortunately, it did not work out that way."

After a short road show, Tom was able to raise a whopping $100 million for his project. Investors were literally climbing all over each other to get into the round. Again from his investor, "Tom's energy was completely infectious and he was swimming in money. Everyone was afraid to miss out on the future. We all overlooked fundamental flaws in his business plan simply because he was such an inspirational person." Tom ran the business for exactly 2 years before running out of money. It turns out that the cost assumptions Tom made about hardware development were off by many factors and, even worse, there were fundamental flaws in his adoption expectations. "Basically, nobody wanted to use his product," the investor recalls. "It just was not a viable enterprise. We were completely taken by his inspirational style, but in the end he did not know how to run a company. I learned a lot about the power, and dangers, of inspirational speaking from this experience!"

Case 3: The Quiet Leader

According to his team, John never cared about accolades or power. "He just wanted to create something great," his COO relayed. "John had no interest in looking good or making money for money's sake. His main focus was creating a company that people loved to work for and that had great products and services. Everything else was secondary." John also had a unique propensity for a CEO: He spoke very quietly and he rarely spoke to large groups. "John was actually quite shy," his COO continued. "He would take people aside and speak to them as if they were his friends. When he was in a small group he would work as if he was simply a member of the team whose role happened to be a leader. I think he sees his leadership role more as a facilitator than a classic leader."

Yet even in his quiet way, John was very inspirational. "He constantly encouraged us to be great," a former employee shared. "Everything he said was focused on creating the best and being the best. I felt like he truly cared about my well-being and my progress." John's interest in others did not stop at his employees. Even his customers found him compelling. Again, from the COO, "John would often quietly call customers and interview them. He would ask them how they are doing, what they are thinking, and what we could do better. They loved him!" In almost every interaction with people, John would leave them smiling and knowing that he cared.

When things got rough in the company during the crash of 2007, John was the first to step in. Without any announcement, John took a pay cut of 75% when sales dropped. "We never knew what he had done until the company was purchased," the COO said. "I still can't believe he did that." During the hardest times John would stay at work and help teams finish a project. Another former employee said, "John would come into the room late at night and ask what he could do to help. We were all totally blown away. I feel almost emotional about it. The guy was not only our CEO, he was a friend who really cared about us. I would do anything for him. Really." After the company was purchased, John wrote checks to every single person in the company to thank them for their service. All his former employees have indicated they would work for John again…in a heartbeat.

CONCLUSION

As I said in the Introduction, creating a company is an incredibly exhilarating process. The challenges are legion…as well as the rewards. You will likely work harder than you have ever worked, and more than once you will wonder why you are doing something so difficult. People who start companies are rarely ever the same after their first startup; taking a 'normal job' seems laughable after the rush of growing something from scratch. Like soldiers back from war, entrepreneurs have a 'look' that only a fellow entrepreneur can see. It is the look that says 'I have been there and know exactly what it is like'. Starting a company is akin to getting a master's degree in business, while at the same time building your own house and having a child. Nothing prepares you for what you are about to experience.

As an entrepreneur it is sometimes best to have what I call 'intelligent naiveté'. You want to be able to think through all the potential problems and outcomes, but not so much that it ruins your desire to start a company. One of the greatest challenges I find with experienced entrepreneurs is that they sometimes know so much about what can go wrong that they get less motivated with every startup. Yes, you will work very hard and come across problems that you never expected…some of them incredibly challenging. Yet this is no reason to worry about all the things that might happen. You must dive into the challenge head-first and trust that anything that comes up will be solvable with a little hard work and crafty thinking. Creating something great is as much about trusting yourself as anything else.

Now that I have warned you about all the challenges, lets talk about the upside. Starting a company will bring you something that a 'regular job' rarely can: Self-actualization. When you build something from the ground up, you push your own boundaries and grow into a larger version of yourself. You literally stretch into a new, more powerful and more competent Self. Yes, the money can be good. So can the feeling of accomplishment. Yet all of that pales in comparison to the feeling of joy you get knowing that you have been tested and have risen to the occasion. Great entrepreneurs are many times very humble and approachable because they don't have anything to prove. Their proof is in what they have experienced and created.

Building a successful company is about building a successful YOU. Learn to identify the roadblocks within yourself, the things that hold you back, and remove them. See how you limit yourself and resolve to break through those limits. Create a vision for your life and your work that inspires you and moves others. Look upward and forward. Dream big, think big and speak big. When you feel an energized and excited feeling inside yourself, you will know you have found your inspiration. Starting a company is not just about business…it is also about growth and creation. Live in a way that is inspired and meaningful.

Perhaps the most exhilarating thing about staring the company is the *process*. Many of the entrepreneurs I coach talk about the stress and strain they feel as they start their company, and yet a few years later they see those days as the most exciting of their lives. Ex-entrepreneurs tell war stories with a glint in their eyes. They smile at the excited newbie's predictions and puffery. Veterans know what the novice can never see: That short of war, starting a company is the wildest, most stressful and most powerful experience they can ever have. As you start down that road to creation, remind yourself to remember these days. Keep pictures and old files. If possible, keep a diary. Trust me, in 5, 10, 20 years you will want to look back and smile.

If you are at all waffling about starting a company, I encourage you to *do it*. Push yourself, stretch into something larger. You can do *anything* to which you put your mind and inspired energy. This bears repeating: If you are inspired to create something and are willing to learn each and every day, then you can do amazing things. This truth is not unique to a gifted few, it is one of the blessings of being human. Everyone on this planet has creative power, we just need to access this power through intention and action. See this in yourself. See your own light and power! Find your own purpose and *create your destiny*.

This life is short. Make something of it.

THE END
(and hopefully YOUR BEGINNING!)

ABOUT THE AUTHOR

K.C. HILDRETH is an entrepreneur, coach and business consultant who has founded or co-founded 8 companies, been a strategy and technology consultant to Fortune 50 telecommunications and financial services companies, and worked for the banking department of a major law firm on Wall Street and Capitol Hill. K.C. was one of the founders of a television technology company that sold for $80 million in 2005 and, in his various career incarnations, has occupied roles including board member, CEO, CTO, COO and investor…as well as salesperson, paralegal and stock-clerk.

K.C. holds a BA in Political Science from Ohio Wesleyan University, an MBA from The University of Virginia Darden School of Business, an MS in Information Systems from The University of Virginia McIntire School of Commerce, and an MA in Spiritual Psychology from the University of Santa Monica. K.C. writes, speaks and works with the deep belief that every person on this planet has a powerful gift, and can choose to use that gift to become greater than they ever imagined.

K.C. lives with his wife in Park City, UT and Manhattan Beach, CA – he can be reached at www.kchildreth.com

www.ingramcontent.com/pod-product-compliance
Lightning Source LLC
Chambersburg PA
CBHW050206230526
45470CB00001B/259